THE COMPLETE
SNOOKER
SHOTS

David Horrix

THE CROWOOD PRESS

First published in 2018 by
The Crowood Press Ltd
Ramsbury, Marlborough
Wiltshire SN8 2HR

enquiries@crowood.com

www.crowood.com

This impression 2023

© David Horrix 2018

All rights reserved. No part of this publication may be reproduced or transmitted in any form or by any means, electronic or mechanical, including photocopy, recording, or any information storage and retrieval system, without permission in writing from the publishers.

British Library Cataloguing-in-Publication Data
A catalogue record for this book is available from the British Library.

ISBN 978 1 78500 357 8

Acknowledgements
My sincere thanks to Neil Selman for his invaluable help in the production of this book.

Typeset by Nova Techset Private Limited, Bengaluru and Chennai
Printed and bound in India by Replika Press Pvt Ltd

Contents

Start at the beginning of the book, regardless of your standard, and work your way through each page, spending more time on the shots that you are finding difficult to master.

Potting the Yellow	7	Pot Yellow with Side	22
Black Red Black	7	Pot Yellow and Stun	23
Pot Red Pot Black	8	Pot Yellow and Screw	23
Red Black Routine	8	Pot Green using Follow, Side,	
Stun-Run Routine	9	Stun and Screw	24
Stun-Screw Routine	9	Pot Brown and Stun to Blue	24
Top to Reds	10	Pot Blue Run Through	25
The Stun and Run Routine	10	Wider Angle on Blue	25
Black to Baulk Routine	11	Pot Blue with Stun/Side	26
Back to Baulk	12	Long-Range Baulk Safety Routine	26
Pot 20 Straight Pinks to Middle	12	Play Safe off the Black	27
Three Straight Reds with Top Routine	13	Straight Long Blues	27
		Safety to Baulk	28
Three Straight Reds with Screw Routine	13	Safety	28
		Green to Black	29
Yellow No Side Routine	14	Black to Yellow	29
Stun to Blue	14	Green to Black	30
Red Right Over the Top Pocket	15	Black to Yellow	30
Red on Black Spot	15	Pack Split	31
The Off-Straight Pink Routine	16	Green Split	31
Pot Almost Straight Blue to Middle	17	Safety off Pink	32
Complete 15 Half-Ball Losers	18	Pot and Screw	32
Pot Yellow off its Spot with a Trace of Left Side	18	Pot Black and Screw to the Cushion	33
Pot Green off its Spot with a Trace of Right Side	19	Pot Red and Screw to Black	33
		Pink to Yellow	34
Safety into the Pack	19	Blue and Stun to Pink	34
Stun-Run	20	Pot Blue and Stun to Brown	35
Stun-Screw	20	Pot Brown and Stun to Blue	35
The Black, Screw, Black Routine	21	Cannon 3 Reds	36
The Pink, Stun, Black Routine	21	Pot Red Stun to Black	36
Black to Black	22	Brown to Black	37

Long Range Baulk Safety	37	Potting Angles Blue to Middle Pocket	60
Back to Baulk	38	Stun-Run into D	61
Double to Baulk	38	Potting Angles on Black into Corner Pocket	61
Stop Shot	39		
3 Cushions and Back	39	Screw Shot Control	62
Pots on Yellow	40	Red to Baulk Colours	62
Pots on the Brown Ball	41	Controlling the Cue Ball	63
Back to Baulk	44	Clearing the Colours	64
Loose Red	45	Pot Green	66
6 Angles on Blue	45	A Final Clearance	68
Pink from 5 Angles	46	Half-Ball Potting	69
Safety First Routine	46	Developing Touch	72
Safe and Sound	47	Pot Blue and Split the Pack	73
Safety in Mind	47	The Break-Off	73
Red off the Top Cushion	48	A Long Pot	74
Baulk Line pots	48	Cross Red Safety	74
Black Safety	49	A Shot to Nothing	75
Red behind Black	49	Yellow into Pack	75
Cue Ball behind Black	50	Safety into the Reds	76
Red/Blue/Colours	50	Blue Close Green	76
Red and Black	51	Swerve and Pot	77
Baulk Safety	51	Safety Shot	77, 78, 79
Safety to Side Cushion	52	Shots to Nothing	79, 80, 81
Thin Red to Black Routine	52	Pot Blue and Split the Pack	82
Stun to Black	53	Half-Ball Safety off the Red	82
Red Screw to Black	53	Safety off a Tempting Red	83
Red Stun to Black	54	Pot Blue and Pink	83, 84
Long Red and Black	54	Safety off Green	84
Long Browns	55	Safety off Blue	85
Pot and Run	55	Safety off Pink	85
Slow Drag	56	Snooker off Green	86
Roll Up Safety Shot	56	Off-Straight Pink	86
Re-Spotted Black Safety Shot	57	Pink and Run	87
Safety to Colours	57	Nearside Pink	87
Pot Black	58	Rest Work	88
Cross Double Safety	58	Pot Red and Blue	88
Black with Top-Spin	59	Stun off Brown	89
Black with Stun	59		
Black with Screw	60		

Run through Green	89
Screw off Yellow	90
Screw off Cushion	90
Escape 1	91
Escape 2	91
Escape 3	92
Escape 4	92
Cocked Hat Shot	93
Cut-Back Doubles	93
The Cross Double	94
Roll-Up Escape	94
Roll Up to Red	95
Ball and Cushion	95
A Shot to Nothing	96
Snooker off the Red	96
Safety off Black	98
1/4 Ball Double	98
Cross Double	99
Double to Middle	99
The Cocked Hat Double	100
Pack Split	100
Green Split	101
Blue Split	101
Split Pack 30	102
The Squeezed Set	102
The T Set	103
Easy Plant	104
Blue from 3 Positions	105
Pink from 3 Positions	106
Stun to Pink	108
Screw to Pink	108
Pink to Middle from 3 Positions	109
Practice on Black	110
A Useful Snooker Shot	112
A Snooker Escape	113
Two Cushion Split	113
Wrong Side of Blue	114
Running Left	114
Screw and Right	115
Black to Yellow	115, 116
Half-Ball Black to Yellow	117
Stun and Side Black to Yellow	117
Straight on Black to Yellow	118
Stun to Yellow from Black	118
Pot Black Left-Hand Side for Yellow	119
Almost Straight to Yellow	119
Wrong Side of Blue to Yellow	120, 121
Pro Safety	121
Safety off Black	125
Safety off Black 2	125
Reply to Safe Black	126
Key Shots on Brown	126
High on Blue	128, 129, 130
Shots on the Pink	131
Pot Black and Screw	132
Pot Pink and Black	132
Pot and Follow	133
Stun Run	133
Screw to Black	134
Easy Safety	134
The Cross Double Safety	135
Position on Black from Green	135
Black to Yellow	136
Pink to Yellow	137
Pot and Cannon	137
Brown to Black	138
Wrong Side of Blue	138, 139
Brown to Blue Shots	140–144
The Complete Shots	144
A Safety Shot	144, 145
Almost Straight	146
Safety – Red to Baulk	146
Safety Double	147
Safety – Loose Red	147
Safety – Red Behind Black	148
Safety – Cue Ball Behind Black	148

Safety – White Behind Black	149	Soft Screw on Black	160
Power Run Through	149	Pot and Run	160
A Trace of Side	150	Black to Yellow	161
A Trace of Side 2	150	Shots from the Opposite Side	162
Angled Red	151	Black to Yellow Shots	164
Potting to the Middle	152	Shots from the Opposite Side	165
Escape Shot	154, 155	Screw with Reverse Side	166
Balls along the Cushion	155, 156	Pink to Yellow Shots	167
Safety on Black	157	From the Opposite Side of the Table	169
Splitting the Pack off Baulk Colours	157	Pink to Yellow Continuation Shots	170
Splitting a Flat Pack	158	From the Opposite Side of the Table	171
Splitting a Pack off the Back Cushion	158		
Blind-Pocket Pot	159		
Fun off the Pink	159	Index	173

Potting the Yellow

Start with the Cue ball 8 inches away from the Green ball.
   Pot 10 Yellows. For beginners just aim to pot one ball from 10 attempts.
   Not an easy shot to start with and needs considerable practice to become consistent; however, once learnt it's a most useful shot to have in your armoury.
   Hit with above-centre striking and play quite gently to get the perfect position for Green (3/4 ball pot).

Black Red Black

Place Black on its spot and Red on the Pink spot.
   Pot Black, gaining a position with a screw shot for the Red. Pot Red and pot the re-spotted Black.
   Beginners just aim to pot a Black then place the White in the best position to pot Red.

Pot Red Pot Black

Place Black on its spot and a Red on the Pink spot.
  Pot the Red with a stun to widen the angle and gain position to pot Black.
  Aim to complete 20 sets of Reds and Blacks.

Red Black Routine

Place a Red on the Pink spot and Black on its spot.
  Pot the Red, running through for position to pot Black.
  Beginners aim to pot Red then place by hand the Cue ball in a good position to pot Black.

Stun-Run Routine

Place a Red on the Blue spot and Black on its spot.

Aim to pot Red and with a stun run-through gain position to pot Black. Below-centre striking is required for this shot and practice is required before you become consistent.

Stun-Screw Routine

Place a Red on the Blue spot and Black on its spot.

Aim to pot Red and with a stun-screw (a very small amount of backspin) shot to gain position to pot Black.

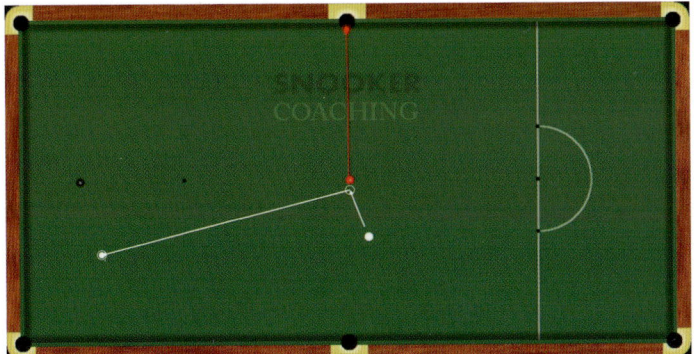

Top to Reds

Pot the Blue ball to the middle and aim to rest the Cue ball opposite the small line of reds.
   Complete five times.

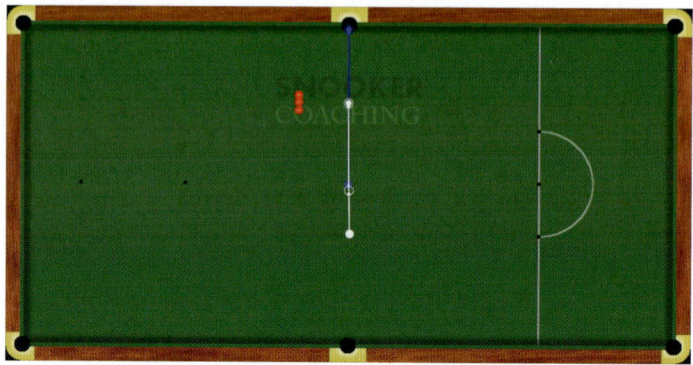

The Stun and Run Routine

Place a Red on the Blue spot. Place Black on its spot.
   With the Cue ball off straight, play a stun run-through shot potting Red and gaining position on Black. Pot Black gaining position to pot Black again.
   Re-spot Black and pot. Continue to pot and re-spot Black and continue until you miss.

Black to Baulk Routine

With Black very close to a top pocket, pot the Black and aim to send the Cue ball into the line of balls in the baulk area.

Use combinations of the screw, stun, top and side to achieve this, and experiment using different power levels and contact points on the line of balls.

Pot straight Black into the top pocket and screw back to the tip three times.

Pot straight Blue into the middle pocket and screw back to the tip three times. Beginners complete one time.

Back to Baulk

Place a triangle of Reds in their normal position.
   Place the Cue ball beneath and to the side of the Reds.
   Clip the end Red of the triangle sending the Cue ball into baulk ensuring that the Cue ball does not cross over the centre line (Black spot to Brown spot).

Pot 20 Straight Pinks to Middle

Pot 20 straight Pinks to the middle absolute dead weight and helped by a Red over the middle to widen the pot.

Three Straight Reds with Top Routine

Pot three straight Reds to the middle pocket with top-spin with the Cue ball following into the same pocket.

Three Straight Reds with Screw Routine

Pot 3 Reds to the middle with a screw with the Cue ball screwing back into the opposite pocket.

13

Yellow No Side Routine

With White near the Green ball pot the Yellow using no side, sending White off the side cushion for position on Green.
   Pot Green and repeat the sequence three times.

Stun to Blue

From the position illustrated, play a stun shot using the side cushion to hold a position on Blue.
   Not the only way to play this shot but one that's important to master.
   Complete the sequence of stunning from Brown to Blue and potting Blue 10 times.

Red Right Over the Top Pocket

From the position illustrated play a drag shot and get position on Black. Pot Black and repeat the sequence three times in succession if you can or just complete three sequences.

Mastering the drag shot is important for accurate position play over long distance, particularly on club cloths.

Red on Black Spot

Place a Red on the Black spot and White at an angle as illustrated. Aim to hit the Red onto the top cushion and into baulk five times.

The Off-Straight Pink Routine

Place Black on its spot and Pink on its spot as illustrated.

Place the Cue ball off straight of Pink so that the natural angle takes the Cue ball away from gaining position on Black.

Play the first shot with left side to come off the cushion to gain position for Black. Pot Black.

Whenever you play any shot with side, it increases the difficulty of the shot, so if you have an option try to avoid playing with side at all costs.

From the same start position practise the same shot as above, but instead of using running side use top and come off both side cushions for position to pot Black.

Pot Almost Straight Blue to Middle

Set the balls as illustrated with the White just a fraction off straight on the Blue. Pot Blue with top-spin, coming off the side cushion for a good position on the Pink ball.

When the angle is slightly bigger, just run through a few inches with the White ball for a good position on the Pink.

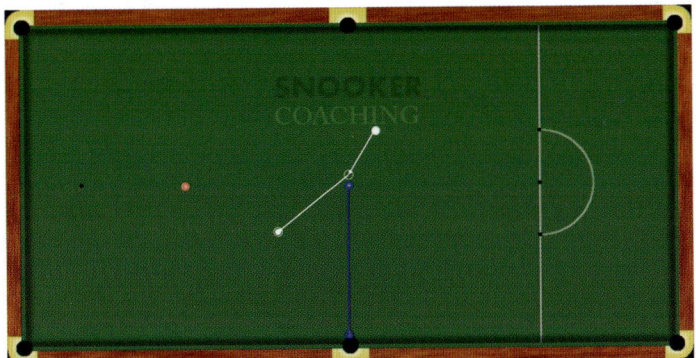

Complete 15 Half-Ball Losers

Set the balls as illustrated with the Yellow ball on the Pink spot and the White ball 3/4 of the way from the middle spot as illustrated.

Your tip is aiming at the edge of the Yellow, and the purpose is for the White to go into the top right-hand pocket as illustrated.

Pot Yellow off its Spot with a Trace of Left Side

Set the balls as illustrated. From this position, you cannot gain position for Green without potting Yellow with a trace of left-hand side to widen the angle off the side cushion. Hit above the middle of the White.

Having potted the Yellow ball also pot the Green and Brown balls to complete the set.

Pot Green off its Spot with a Trace of Right Side

Similar shot to the previous one but this time a trace of right-hand side is needed to gain position on the Brown. Pot the Brown ball to complete the set.

Safety into the Pack

Set all of the balls up as illustrated.
  Place the Cue ball a couple of inches behind Brown.
  Aim to hit below the middle pocket then off the top cushion with the Cue ball resting on the second Red in from the right as you look at the bottom of the pack.

Stun-Run

Place Blue on its spot and Black on its spot.
 Aim to pot Blue and with a stun run through to gain position to pot Black, which you then pot.

Stun-Screw

Place Blue and Black on their spots as illustrated.
 Aim to pot Blue with a screw shot to gain position to pot Black.

The Black, Screw, Black Routine

Place Black and Pink on their spots as illustrated and the White ball a fraction lower than the Black ball.
 Pot the Black, gaining position on the Pink ball with a screw shot.
 Pot the Pink ball and then repeat.

The Pink, Stun, Black Routine

Place Black and Pink on their spots as illustrated.
 Pot the Pink with a stun shot to widen the angle and gain position to pot the Black ball.
 Repeat the sequence of shots.

Black to Black

Place the Cue ball below the middle pocket as illustrated in the diagram.

Place the Black in a straight line with the Cue as illustrated.

Aim to hit the Black into the middle area behind the Black spot resting against one of the Reds, which is harder than it looks and requires a good judgement of pace.

Pot Yellow with Side

Set the balls as illustrated. This time, to gain position for Green you need to use just a trace of left-hand side to widen the angle as the White ball comes off the side cushion. A proficient player very rarely misses this sort of shot, but it does require practice.

Pot Yellow and Stun

Place the balls as illustrated, but this time, the White ball is even further out than on the previous shot.

No amount of side will let you get position for the Green ball so, this time, you need to play a stun shot to gain a good position on the Green ball.

Pot Yellow and Screw

Set the balls as illustrated in the diagram.

This time the White ball and Yellow ball are almost in a straight line, so it's a screw shot that's required to gain a good position on the Green ball.

Pot Green using Follow, Side, Stun and Screw

These are almost the same shots that you played on the Yellow ball, but this time, it is potting the Green ball to gain position for the Brown ball. You can see from the diagram that the start points are indicated by the White ball and the Xs. The first shot is just a simple pot with no side and hitting gently and above the centre of the White ball. The next shot is using a trace of right-hand side to widen the angle on the shot. The next shot is a stun shot, and the final shot is a screw shot.

Pot Brown and Stun to Blue

Set the balls as illustrated in the diagram.

From this position, you can play a stun shot to pot the Brown ball and come off the side cushion to hold the position for the Blue ball.

24

Pot Blue Run Through

Set the balls as illustrated with the White ball almost straight with the Blue ball.
   Nothing complicated here and despite being almost straight you can still pot the Blue and hitting above the centre of the White ball run through and off the side cushion for position on the Pink ball.

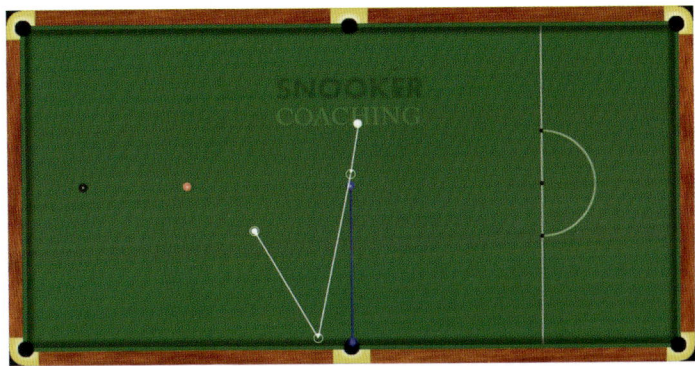

Wider Angle on Blue

Set the balls as illustrated and this time, there is a slightly wider angle between the White and Blue balls.
   Still an easy shot as from this position you can pot Blue and just allow the White ball to travel a few inches for a good position on the Pink ball.
   This is a basic shot that all proficient players are adept at playing.

Pot Blue with Stun/Side

Set the balls as illustrated with the angle now even wider than on the previous shot.

This sort of shot becomes much harder as you need to play a stun shot, but you also need to play the shot with right-hand side to check the Cue ball off the top cushion to gain position on the Pink ball.

This is a basic shot that all proficient players are adept at playing.

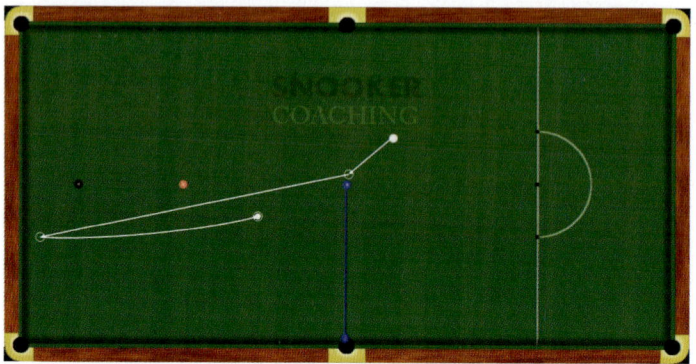

Long-Range Baulk Safety Routine

Set up all the balls as shown in the diagram.

Aim to send the Cue ball into the baulk area and safe. Quite easy but requiring practice.

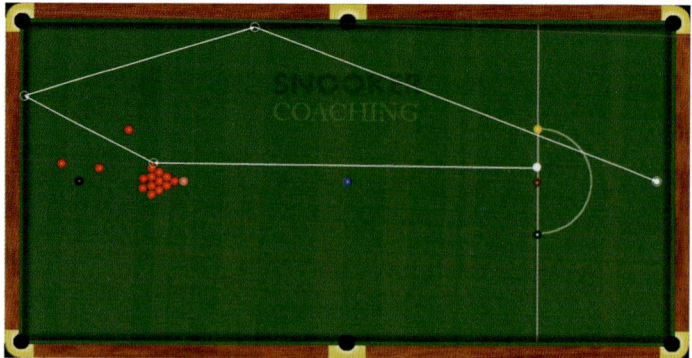

Play Safe off the Black

Set the balls as illustrated.
 Great little exercise for developing touch; try to make a wafer-thin contact off the black so that the Black ball hardly moves and the shot can be achieved by the most gentle of strokes.

Straight Long Blues

Set the balls as illustrated with the Blue ball and the White ball in a perfectly straight line.
 Aim to pot the Blue ball into the top pocket and for this shot strike the White ball below the centre.

Safety to Baulk

Set up all the balls as illustrated in the diagram.
　Aim to double the Red ball behind Black and to send the Cue ball into baulk and safe.

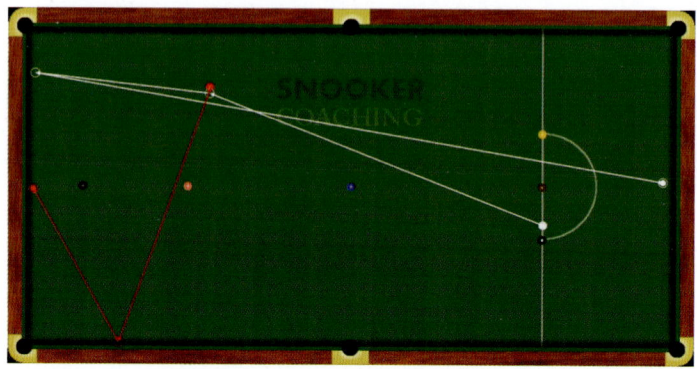

Safety

Set up all the balls as illustrated in the diagram.
　Aim to send the Cue ball into baulk and safe and placing the Red ball into a safe position on the side cushion.
　Your priority on this shot is to ensure the White ball finishes in the baulk area.

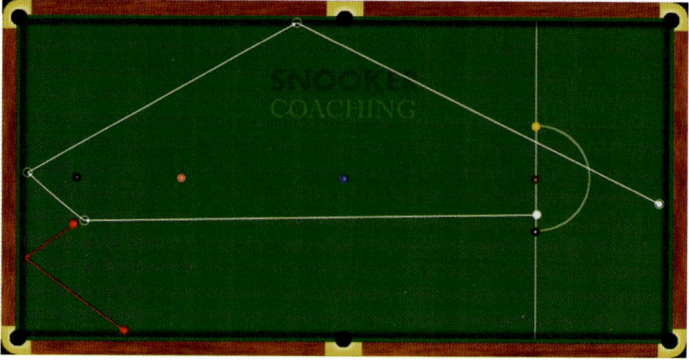

Green to Black

Set up all the balls as shown in the diagram.
   Aim to pot Green, sending the Cue ball off two cushions gaining position to pot Black.

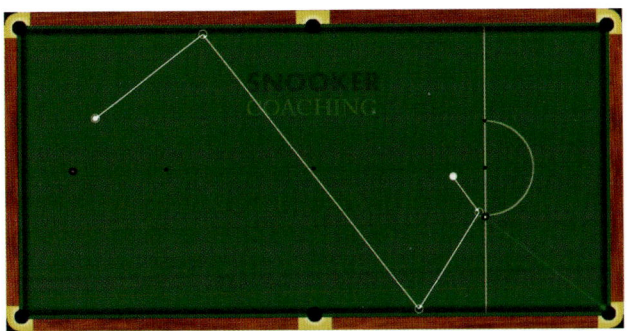

Black to Yellow

Set up the balls as shown in the first diagram below. Aim to pot Black with a stun shot and gaining position to pot Yellow. From the slightly straighter position in the second diagram, run through off two cushions as indicated.

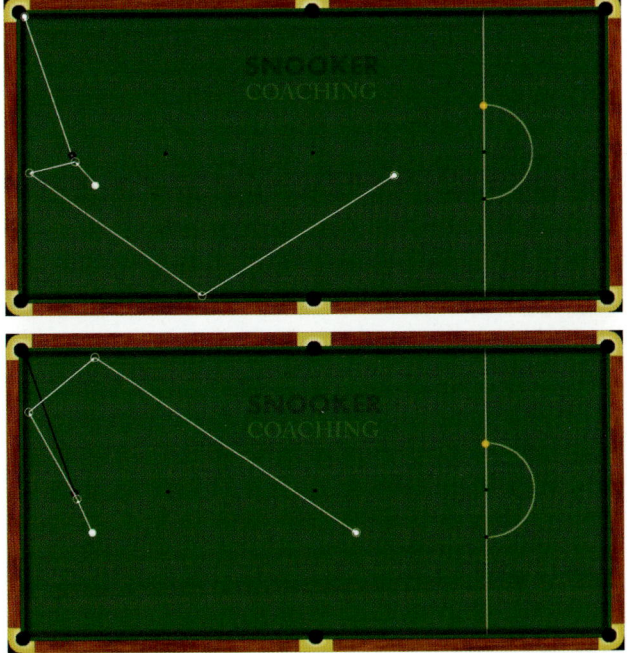

Green to Black

Set up all the balls as shown in the diagram. You have practised this shot before so it should be easier now.

Aim to pot Green, sending the Cue ball off two cushions gaining position to pot Black.

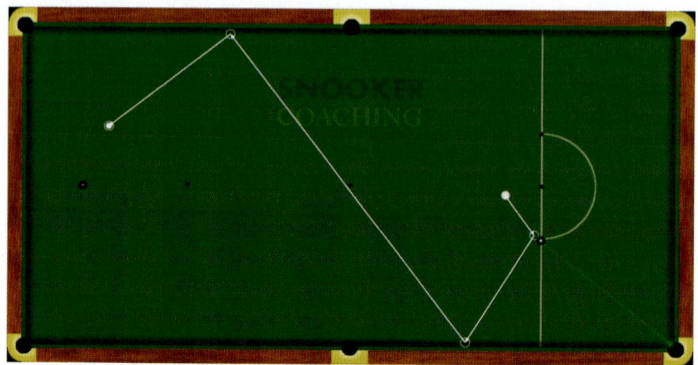

Black to Yellow

You have practised this so it should be easier now. Set up the balls as shown in the first diagram below. Aim to pot Black with a stun shot and gaining position to pot Yellow. From the slightly straighter position in the second diagram, run through off two cushions as indicated.

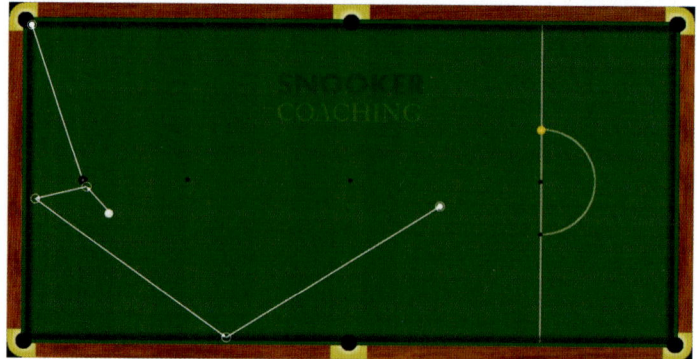

Pack Split

This is not an easy shot. You must pot the Yellow ball and at least make some contact with the pack on every attempt at this exercise. Running side (left) required.

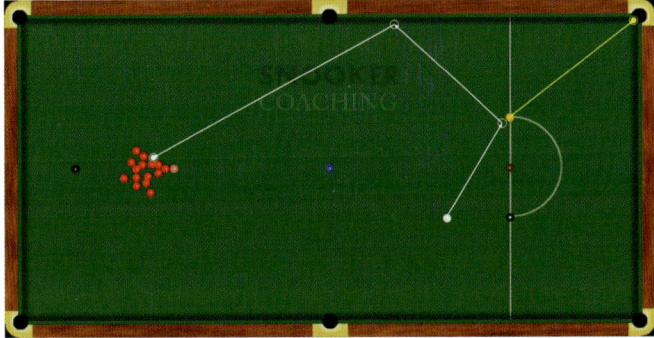

Green Split

Again, not an easy shot. You must at least make the pot and contact with the pack. Running side (right) needed here.

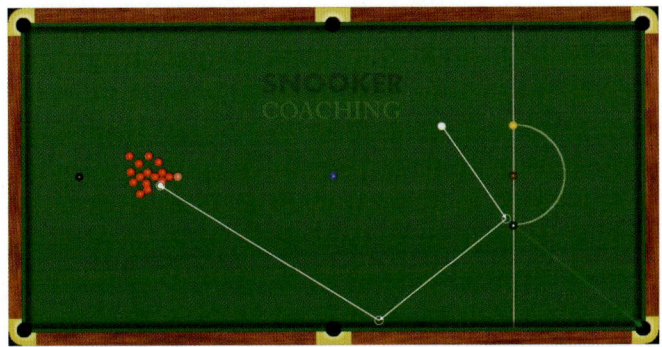

Safety off Pink

Set the balls as illustrated.
   Aim to hit above the centre of the White ball and make a wafer-thin contact on the Pink ball to send the White ball into baulk and near to the bottom cushion.

Pot and Screw

Set the balls as illustrated with the White and Blue balls in a perfectly straight line with the middle pocket.
   Aim to pot the Blue ball and screw the White ball back into the opposite pocket.

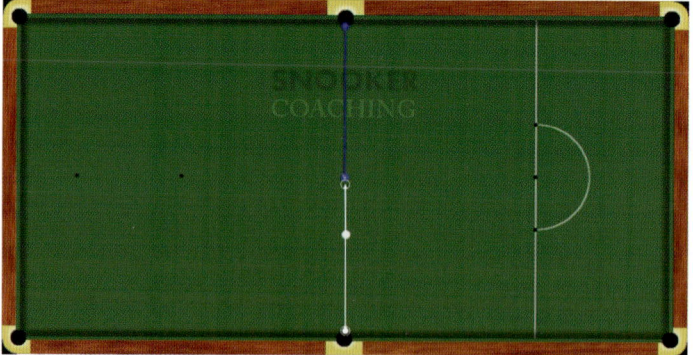

Pot Black and Screw to the Cushion

Set the balls as illustrated with the top pocket, Black ball and the White ball in a perfectly straight line with each other.
 Try to pot the straight Black and screw back to the side cushion.

Pot Red and Screw to Black

Set the balls as illustrated.
 Pot the Red ball into the Yellow pocket and screw the White ball up the table for position on the Black ball, which you pot.

Pink to Yellow

Place Pink and Yellow on their spots as illustrated.
  Place the Cue ball as illustrated.
  Aim to pot Pink gaining position on the Yellow, and for the first few shots observe the path of the White ball when struck at various heights. After some experimentation, you will find which height and pace you need to use to get the White ball to follow the line indicated on the diagram.

Blue and Stun to Pink

Place the balls as illustrated in the diagram.
  Striking below the centre, aim to pot the Blue ball and then hit the Pink ball full in the face with the White ball. This is achieved by playing a stun shot and is an essential part of controlling the White ball.

Pot Blue and Stun to Brown

Place the balls as illustrated in the diagram.
Pot the Blue ball and stun into the Brown ball.
Not too hard and once you know the correct height and power to achieve the shot, you will find this quite easy.

Pot Brown and Stun to Blue

Set the balls as illustrated in the diagram.
Aim to pot the Brown ball, stunning off the side cushion and then making gentle contact with the Blue ball.

Cannon 3 Reds

Place 3 Reds on the side cushion as illustrated.
Place Blue on its spot and Cue ball as illustrated.
Aim to pot Blue and cannon into the first Red (once done remove the Red).
Continue from the start position and aim to cannon the second Red.
Continue and cannon the third Red.

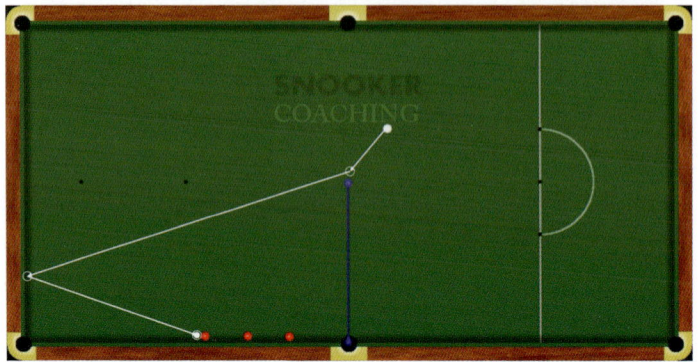

Pot Red Stun to Black

A nice easy routine but still one that requires concentration. Simply pot the Red with a stun shot to gain position on the Black ball, which you also must pot to complete the combination.

Brown to Black

Place Brown and Black on their spots as illustrated in the diagram.
   Position the Cue ball as illustrated.
   Pot Brown, gaining position to pot Black, which you must do to complete a set.

Long Range Baulk Safety

Set up all the balls as shown in the diagram.
   Aim to send the Cue ball into baulk and safe.

Back to Baulk

Place balls as illustrated in the diagram.
 Aim to send the Cue ball into baulk and the Red into a safe position as illustrated.

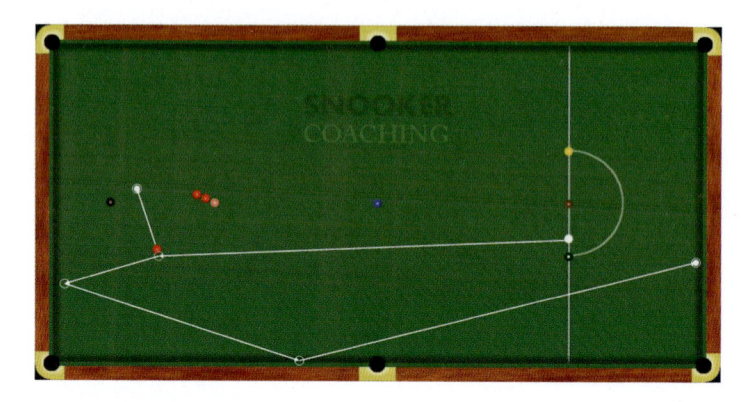

Double to Baulk

Set balls as illustrated.
 Attempt to double the Red behind Black, sending the Cue ball into baulk.

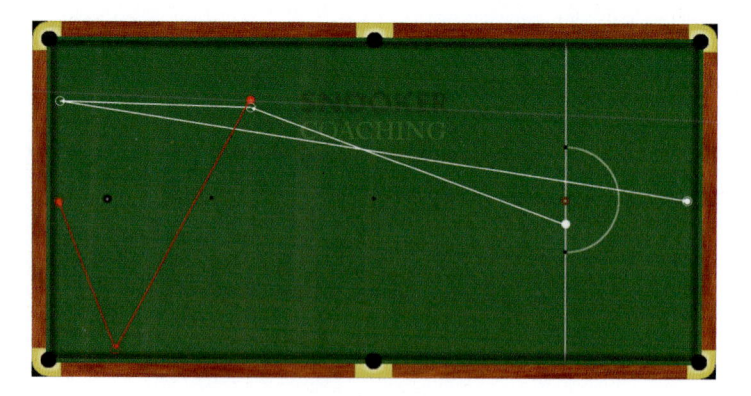

Stop Shot

Place the balls as illustrated with the top pocket, Red and White balls in a straight line. Strike low and with power to stop the White ball dead. Pot the Black ball to complete the set.

3 Cushions and Back

Hit White off three cushions and back to baulk. This is about feel and touch and one that's easy but catches out even the best players.

Pots on Yellow

Detailed below are the different positions from which to pot the Yellow ball. These are very basic shots that all proficient players can play with comfort.

Complete each shot five times; these shots have been practised previously. The first shot needs to be hit above the centre with no side to gain position for a ¾ Ball Green. From each position try not to stray beyond the area indicated by the reds, as this will make your shot on the Green easier.

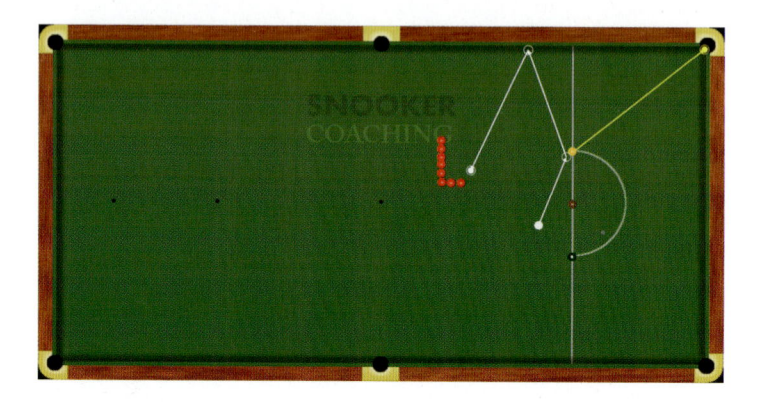

The second shot has the White ball further away, so to gain position on the Green ball requires a trace of left-side to widen the angle off the side cushion.

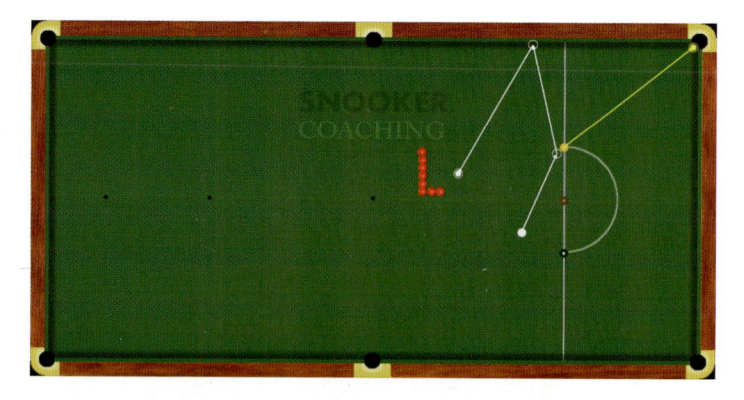

Shot 3 (opposite above) has the White ball even further out, so a firm stun shot is needed to come off the side cushion for position on Green.

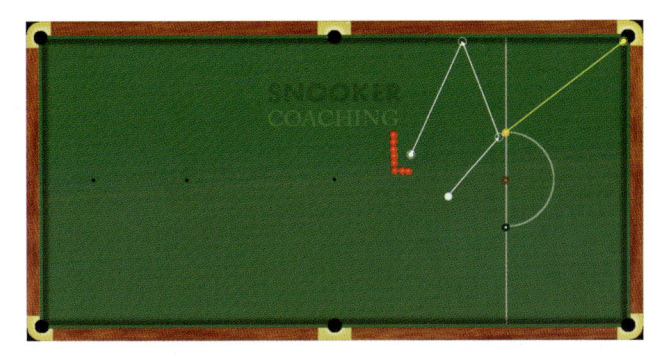

The fourth shot when straight is a simple screw shot.

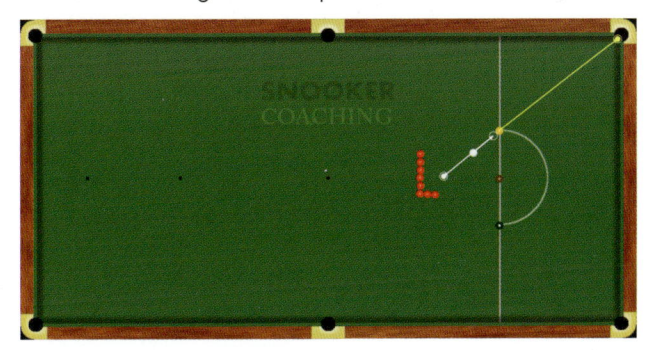

Pots on the Brown Ball

Detailed below are various very well-known positions on the Brown ball. Proficient players know and practise these shots, which is why you rarely see them missing from any of these positions.

Complete each shot five times.

Beginners complete each shot twice.

The first shot is from a dead-straight position, so it's a simple screw shot off the side cushion.

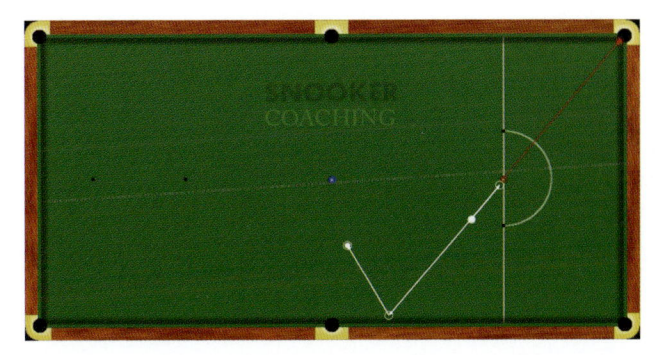

Shot 2 is a 3/4 ball pot and can be played in at least two ways. The first way is a pot and screw shot for position on the Blue ball. The second way is a forcing stun shot for position on the other side of Blue without touching a cushion.

Spend about 10 minutes on this exercise.

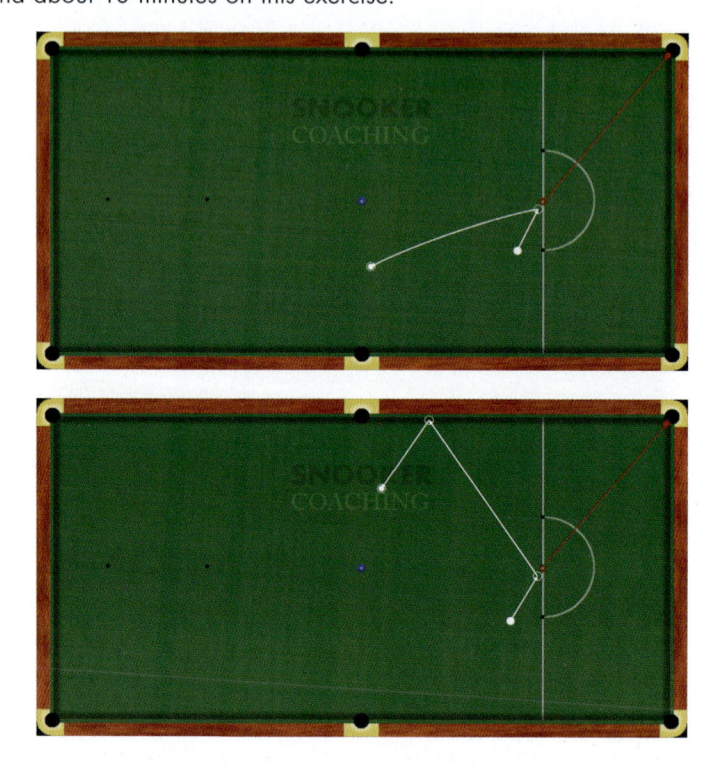

Shot 3 is about a half-ball pot, so no side is needed for a simple stun shot off the cushion holding position for the Blue ball.

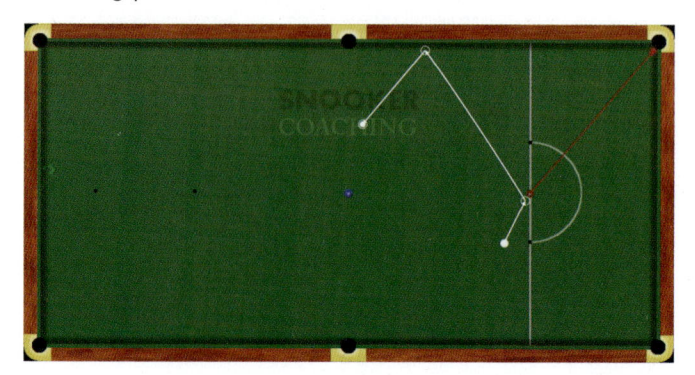

Shot 4 is about a 1/4 ball pot and requires a very delicate screw shot to gain a good position on the Blue ball. Tough, but worth practising.

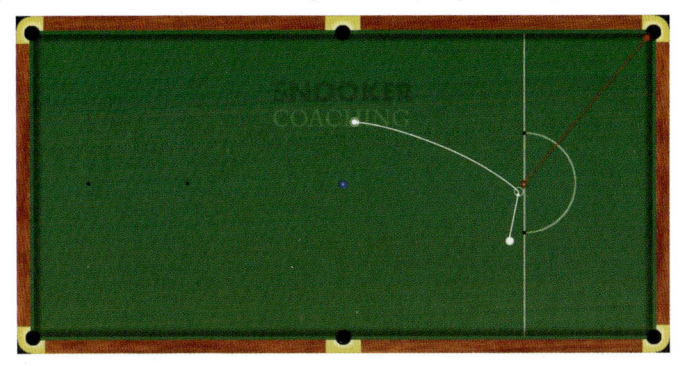

Shot 5 is now a 3/4 ball pot and requires a trace of running side (left) to gain position off the side cushion for the Blue ball.

Shot 6 will probably require the rest to make this one. Quite easy, a simple pot with a stun shot to come off the bottom and side cushion and holding position for the Blue ball.

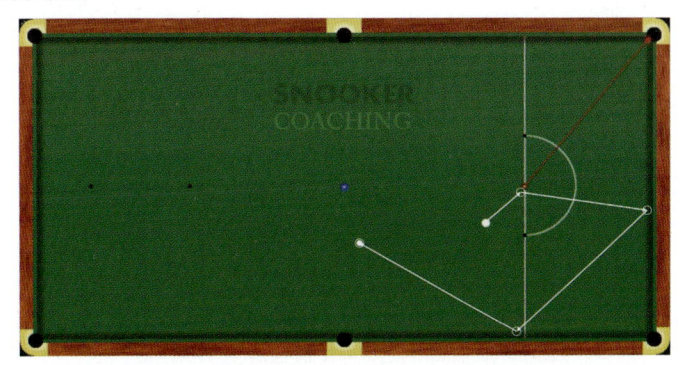

Shot 7 again will require the use of a rest and is about a 1/4 ball pot. No side needed for this one and striking about the centre of the White ball and not too hard to gain position for the Blue ball.

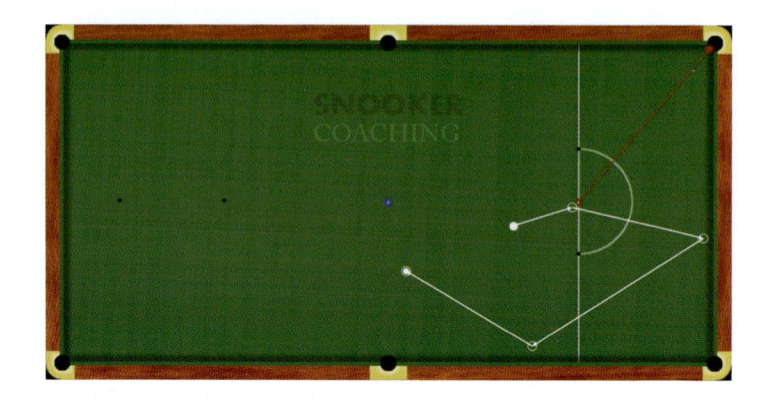

Back to Baulk

Set balls as illustrated.

From the Cue ball, start positions aim to send the Cue ball off the pack and into baulk.

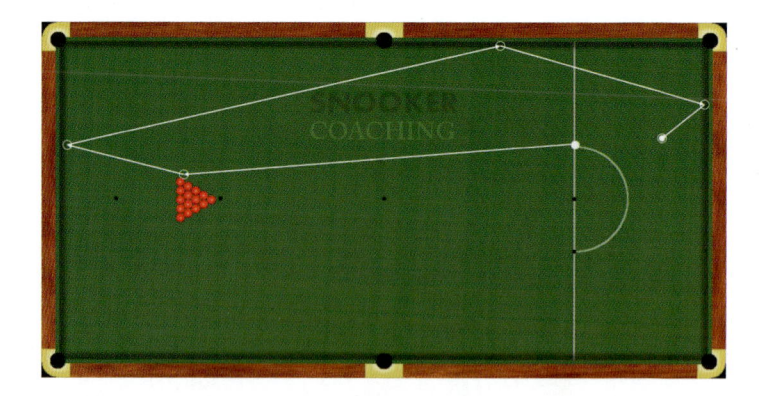

Loose Red

Set balls as illustrated.

Aim to hit the loose Red on the top cushion and do this with just enough pace to contact the Red.

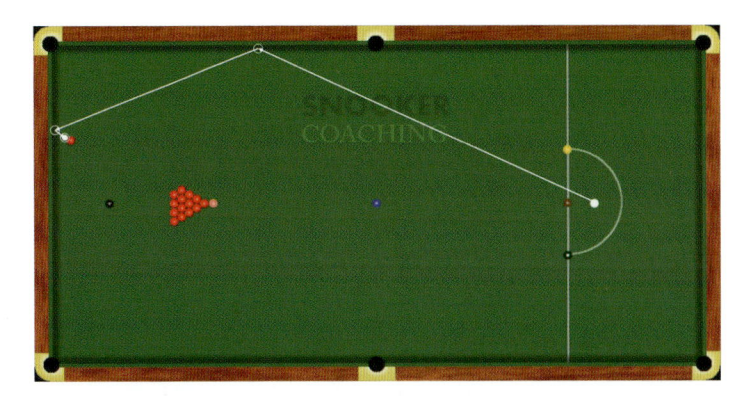

6 Angles on Blue

Set the balls as illustrated using the Red balls as markers and to be replaced by the White ball and with no side when playing the actual shot. Simply pot the Blue ball to the middle pocket from 5 different angles by hitting high on the White ball. As well as potting the Blue ball, try to get the White ball to finish in the baulk area from each shot.

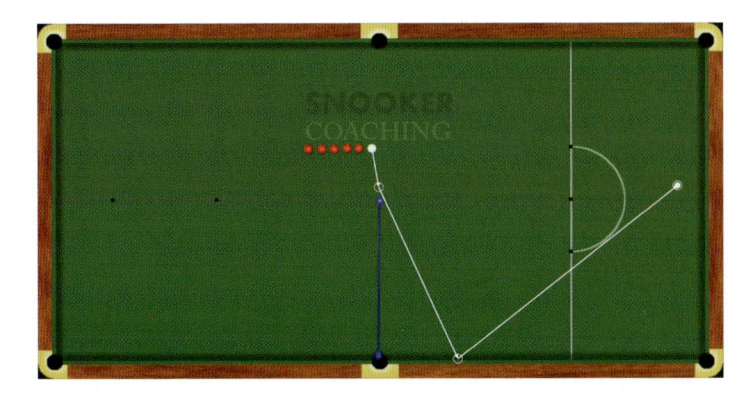

45

Pink from 5 Angles

Pot the Pink ball into the top pocket from each of the positions indicated by the White and Red ball in the diagram.

Hit each shot with top-spin and after potting the Pink simply observe the path that the White ball takes.

These pots are not easy, but they are quite achievable; however, the main thing is the learning from observing the course of the White ball.

Safety First Routine

Place balls as illustrated.

Aim to come off the pack and into the area in baulk and behind Green. If you manage from the position indicated then start from other positions in the D.

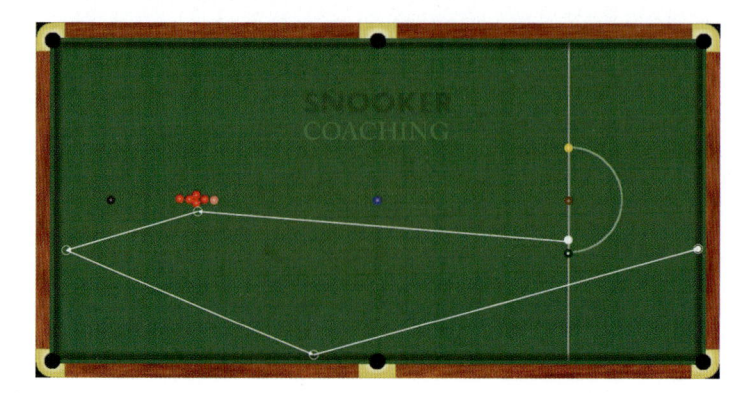

Safe and Sound

Place balls as illustrated.
   Aim to hit the Yellow off the side cushion and into baulk and the White ball on or near the top cushion.

Safety in Mind

Place balls as illustrated.
   Put Red into a safe position and the Cue ball onto the top cushion behind Black.

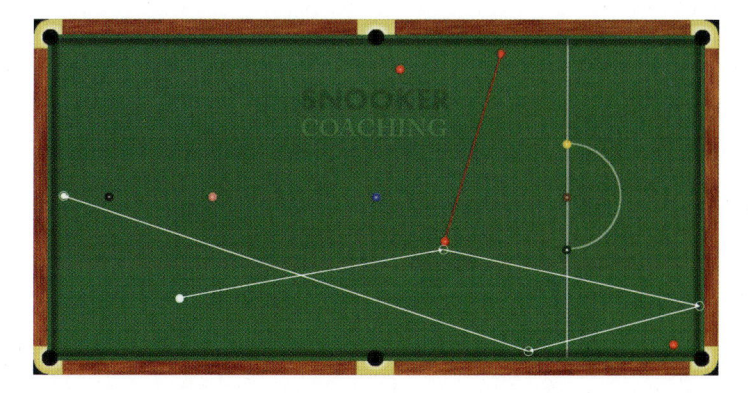

Red off The Top Cushion

With the Reds over Yellow and Green pockets and White in the D, pot the Reds by going up and down the table.

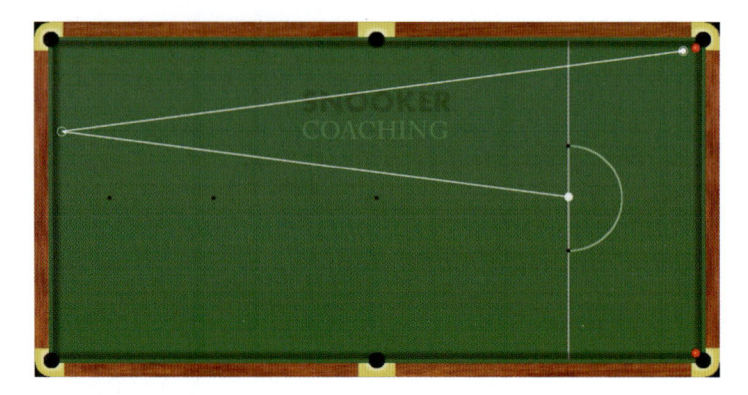

Baulk Line Pots

Set balls as illustrated in the diagram.
   Starting from the Pink spot, try to pot the reds into the bottom pockets. Play until you are consistent with the shots.

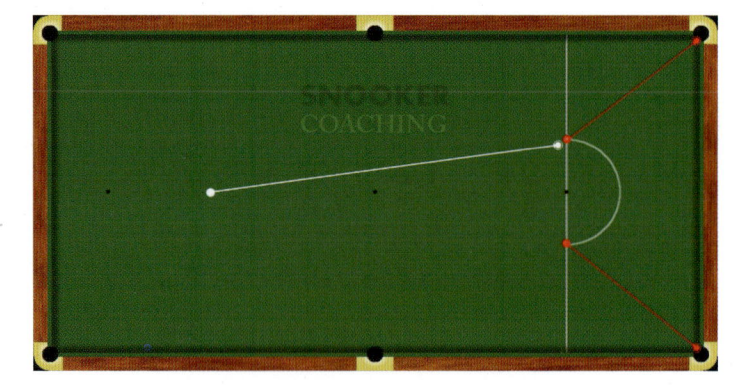

Black Safety

Set the balls as illustrated.
   Aim to send the Cue ball in behind Black and Red into baulk.

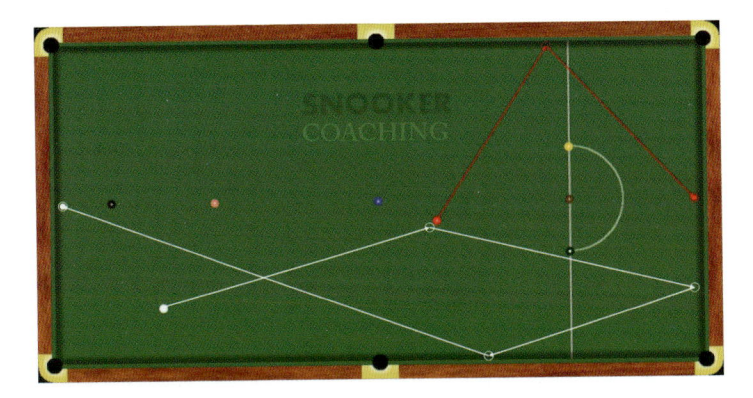

Red behind Black

Set the balls as illustrated.
   Aim to send the Red ball in behind Black and the White ball into baulk.

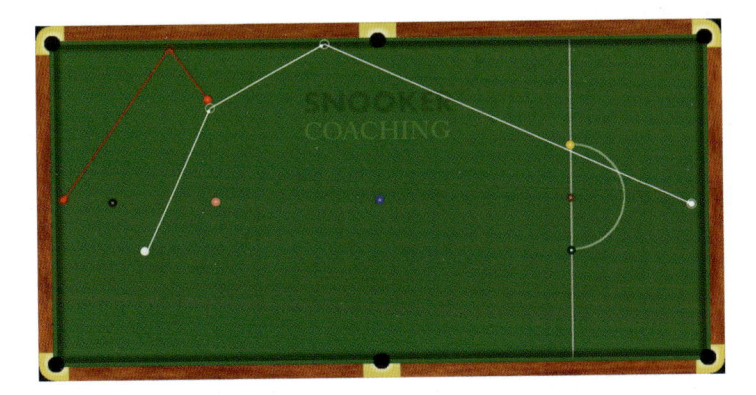

Cue Ball behind Black

Set the balls as illustrated.
   Aim to send the Cue ball in behind Black and the Red ball into baulk.

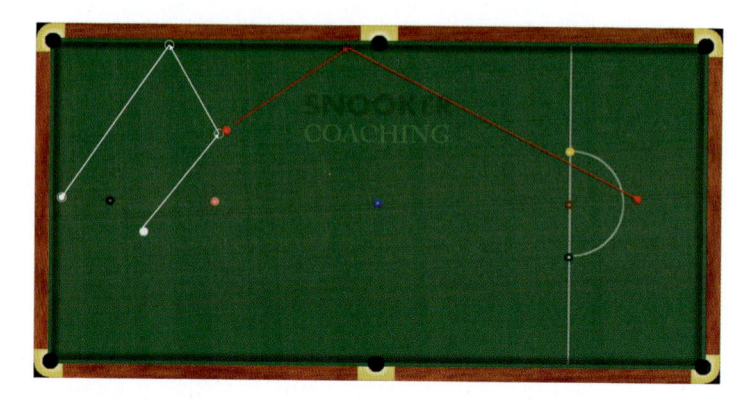

Red/Blue/Colours

Set the balls as illustrated.
   Aim to pot Red, gaining position to pot Blue and then try to clear the colours.

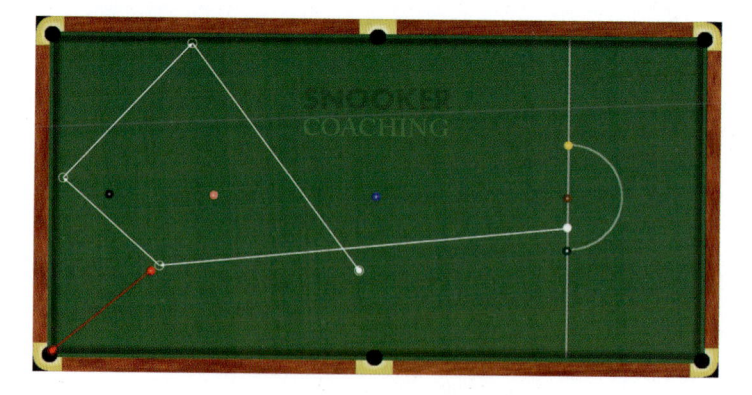

Red and Black

Set the balls as illustrated.
   Aim to pot Red, gaining position to pot Black.
   Pot the Black ball to complete the set.

Baulk Safety

Set the balls as illustrated.
   Aim to come off the pack and into baulk and as close as possible to the position indicated in the diagram.

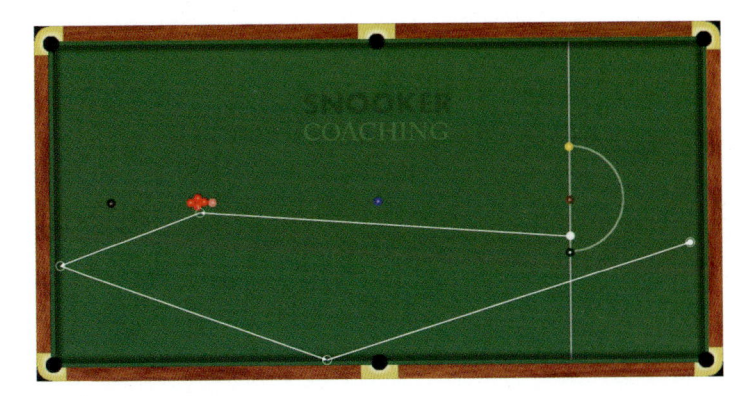

Safety to Side Cushion

Set the balls as illustrated.
   With the Red ball on the Black spot and the White ball starting from the Green spot, aim to send the Red ball beyond the middle pocket and close to the side cushion for safety.

Thin Red to Black Routine

Set the balls as illustrated.
   Aim to send the Cue ball thin off the Red and behind Black. This is a tough shot but well worth spending time practising.

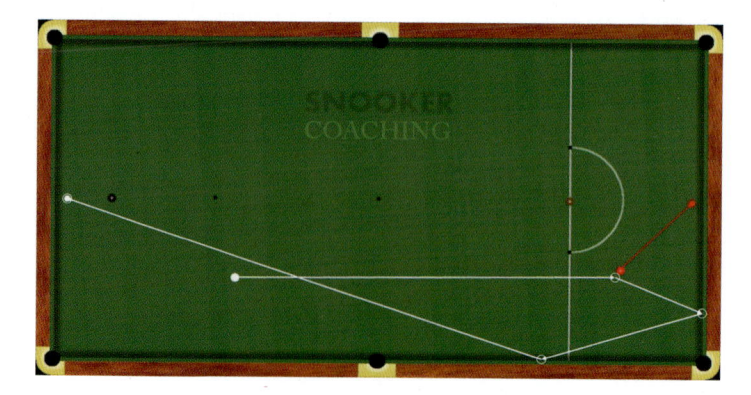

Stun to Black

Set the balls as illustrated.
   Aim to pot the long Red, stunning off the side cushion for position on Black. Pot the Black ball then clear the colours in sequence.

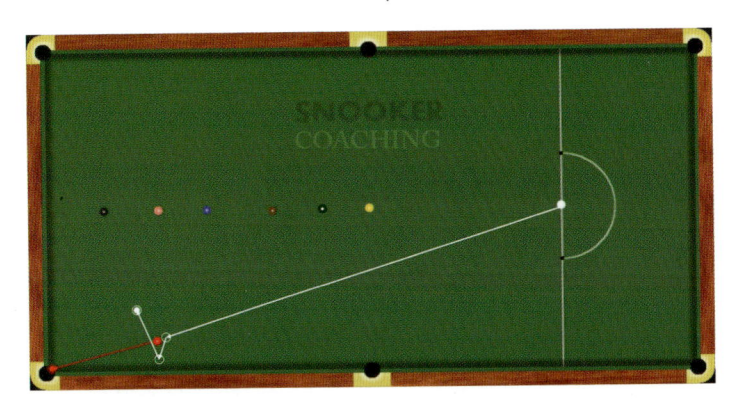

Red Screw to Black

Set the balls as illustrated.
   Aim to pot the long Red, screwing back for position on Black.

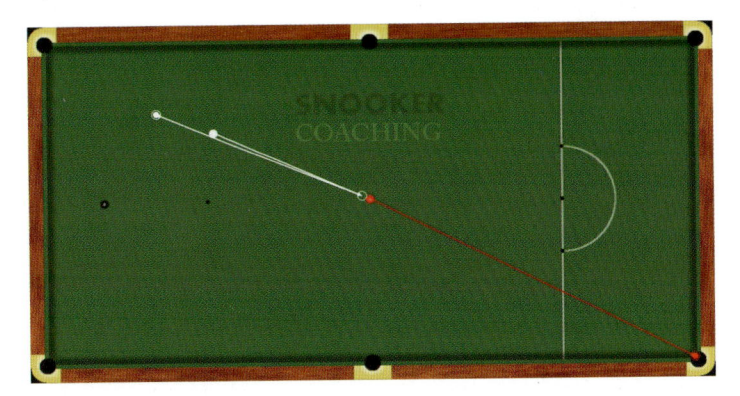

Red Stun to Black

Pot the Red ball, stunning for position on the Black ball, which you pot to complete the set.

If you can become consistent with this shot you will be a better player.

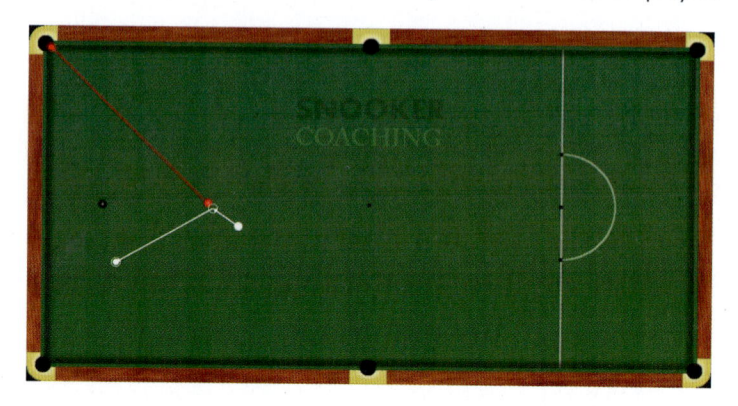

Long Red and Black

Set the balls as illustrated.

Aim to pot the long Red holding for position on Black, which you must pot to complete the set.

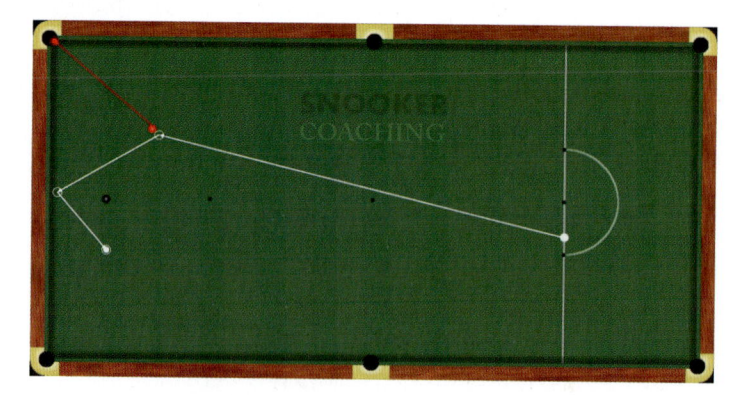

Long Browns

Set the balls as illustrated in the diagram.
   Aim to pot the long Brown from the position shown in the diagram.
   Complete 10 times.

Pot and Run

Set the balls as illustrated in the diagram.
   Aim to pot the long Red, running off two cushions for position on Black.
   Pot the Black ball to complete the set.

Slow Drag

Play a slow drag shot to move the Green ball gently a very short distance, snookering your opponent on both Reds over the top pockets.

Be careful with this shot: virtually every player has tried this and fallen short at some point in their playing career!

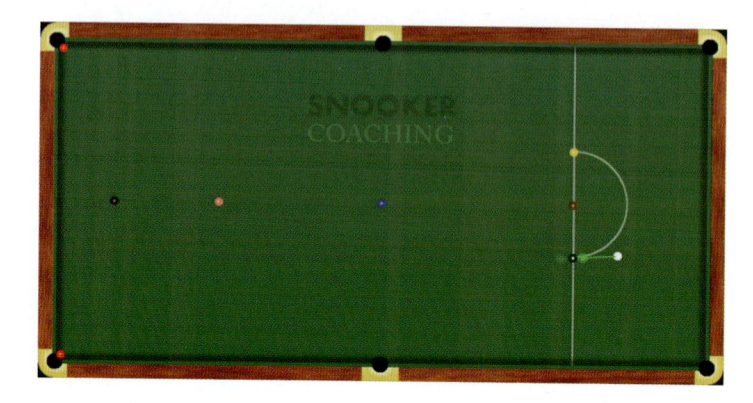

Roll Up Safety Shot

Like the last shot but instead of a drag shot hit high on the White ball to gently roll onto the Green ball, again snookering your opponent on both Reds over the pocket.

Be careful with this shot: virtually every player has tried this and fallen short at some point in their playing career!

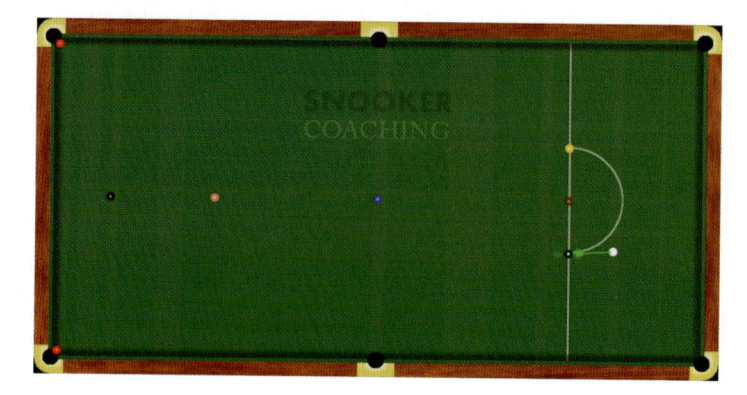

Re-Spotted Black Safety Shot

For this important shot play a drag shot to control both balls onto opposite side cushions.

Safety to Colours

Starting from anywhere in between the Brown and Green spots, aim to contact the Red ball and return the White ball into baulk, and make gentle contact with the line of colours. Once you have got the pace, then aim for specific colours in the line.

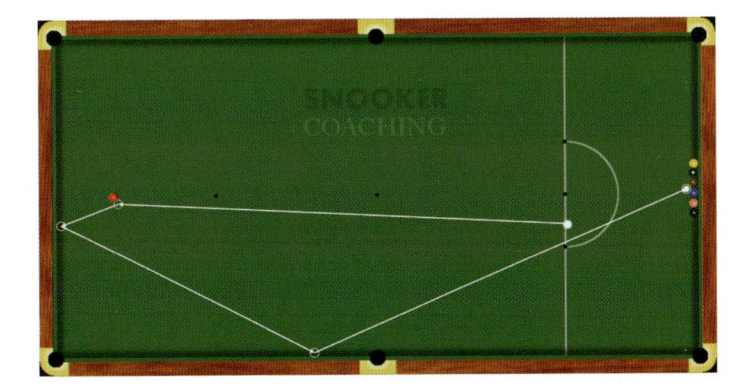

Pot Black

Pot a straight Black from the start point illustrated in the diagram by the White ball. Use top-spin and observe the path of the White ball after potting the Black ball.

Move the White ball one ball's width higher (replace the Red ball with the White ball) and again pot the Black ball using top-spin and observe the path of the White ball.

Repeat from each of the positions, potting the Black ball with top-spin and observing the path of the White ball.

Cross Double Safety

From the position illustrated, send the Red close to the top cushion and white into the baulk area.

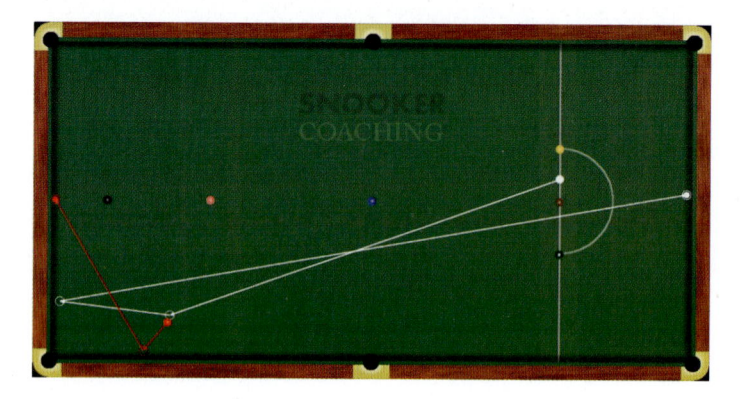

Black with Top-Spin

From the position illustrated, pot the Black ball with top-spin so that the Black just drops in and the white moves the minimum distance without contacting the reds.
    An excellent exercise for developing touch and one I have used for many years with all my students.

Black with Stun

From the position illustrated pot the Black ball with a stun shot so that the White ball moves the minimum distance possible without contacting the reds.

Black with Screw

From the position illustrated pot the Black ball with a screw shot so that the White ball moves the minimum distance possible without contacting the reds.

An excellent exercise for developing touch and one I have used for many years with all my students.

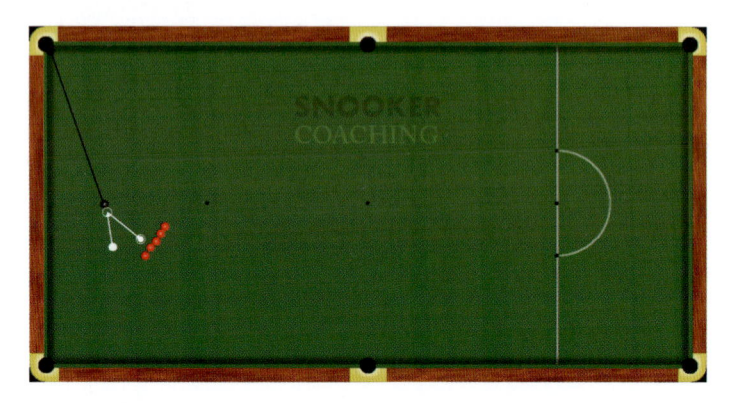

Potting Angles Blue to Middle Pocket

Place Blue on its spot and a Red 18 inches from the Blue, making a full-ball pot into the centre pocket. Place 3 Reds either side of the white as illustrated or all 1 1/2 ball widths apart.

Starting with the full-ball potting angle, aim to pot the Blue using medium pace and plain ball striking. Repeat this on the remaining 6 Reds. Replacing the Red ball with the white ball will give 3/4, 1/2 and 1/4 ball potting angles from both sides of the Blue.

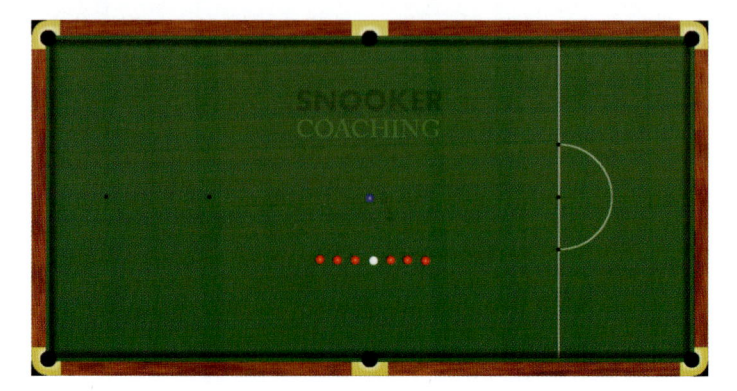

Stun-Run into D

Use all the balls for this exercise.
    Set the object ball in a straight line with the Yellow pocket. Use a Stun-Run through shot and aim to pot the ball and finish with the cue ball inside the D.
    See if you can complete the exercise without missing!

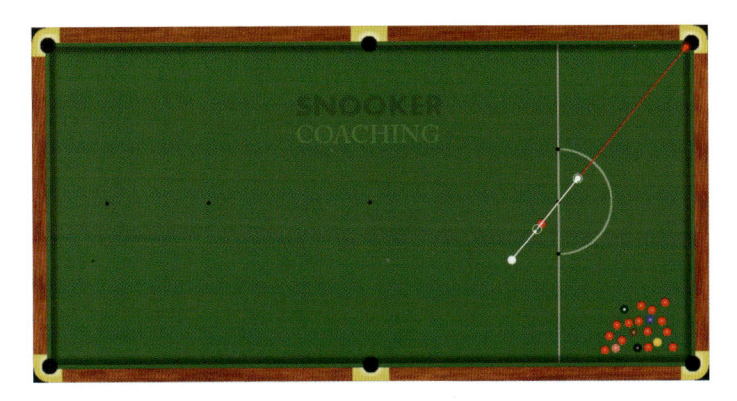

Potting Angles on Black into Corner Pocket

Place a Black on its spot and the white in line and 18 inches from the Black. Place 3 Reds either side as illustrated and with 1 1/2 ball's width between each Red.
    Start with the straight pot on Black then pot the Black from each of the remaining positions that the Reds are in.
    Repeat from both sides of the table.

Screw Shot Control

Set balls as illustrated.
 Start at the position indicated and using a screw and a touch of right-hand side practise screwing the Cue ball in the pocket.
 Complete three successful screw shots from this position.

Red to Baulk Colours

This is a thin angle on the Red ball, so you need to use both cushions as illustrated to gain position on any baulk colour. Ensure you do not travel beyond the baulk-line.
 After potting any baulk colour then aim to clear the colours as normal.

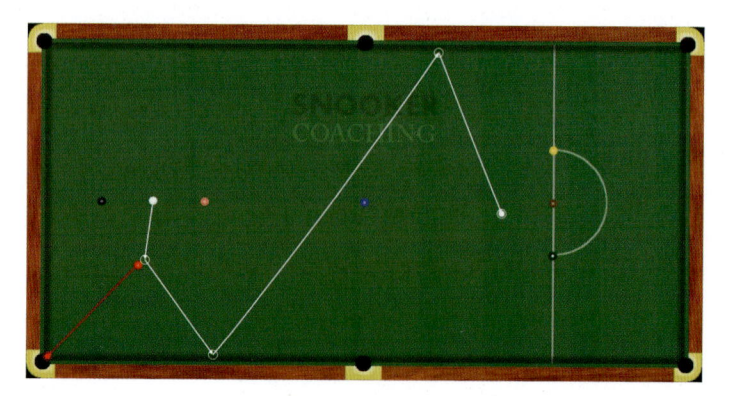

Controlling the Cue Ball

Place a Red on the Pink spot. Place the Cue ball as illustrated and pot Black, gaining position to pot the Red into the top pocket. Strike central and play with just a trace of left-hand side to bring the Cue ball into a potting position.

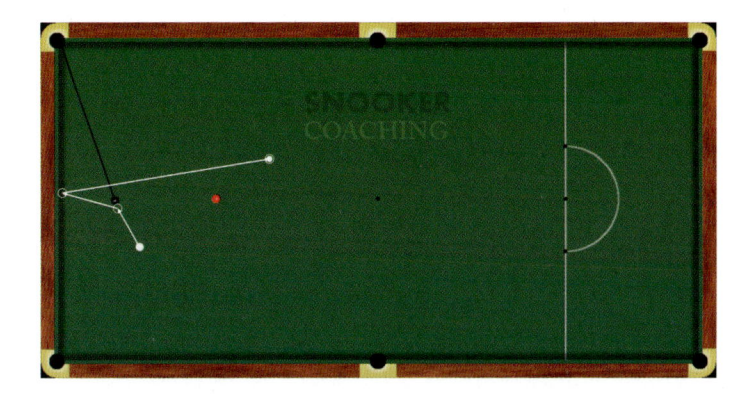

This time use strong right-hand side from an off-straight position to gain position for Red to top pocket.
Try to pot the Red!

Clearing the Colours

Set the balls as illustrated and practise gaining the exact position shown in each colour.

Don't continue onto the next colour until you have gained perfect position off the pot you are going for.

Complete three clearances.

The first shot – from about a 3/4 ball angle on the Yellow screw back for position on the Green ball, which is ideally a 3/4 ball pot.

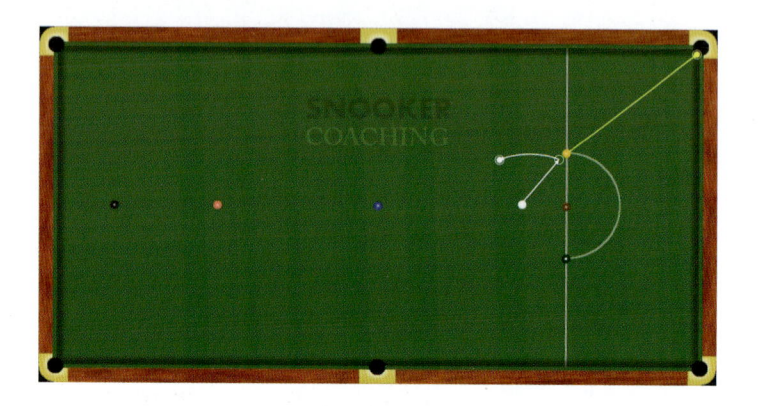

The Second shot – from this 3/4 ball pot on the Green ball play a screw shot to leave anything between a 1/2 ball and a 3/4 ball pot on the Brown ball.

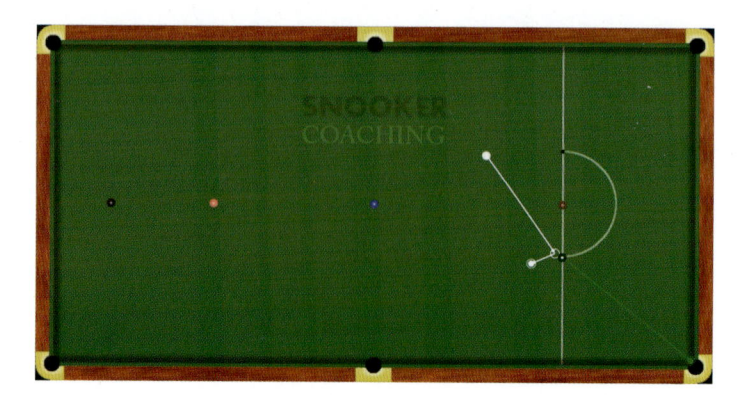

The Third shot – from almost a 1/2 ball on the Brown ball aim to stun off the cushion to leave a 3/4 ball pot on the Blue ball.

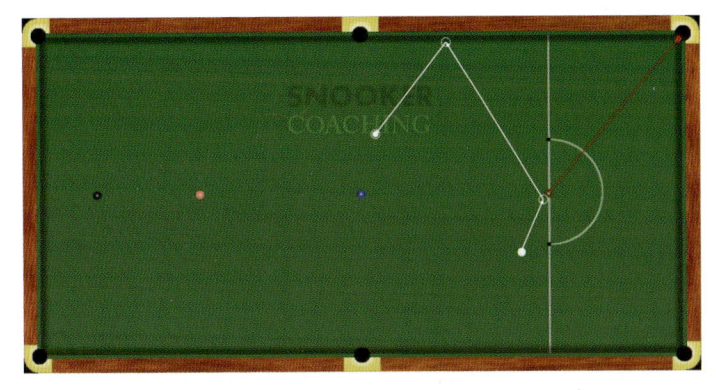

The Fourth shot – easy pot on the Blue ball running through for a 3/4 ball position on the Pink ball.

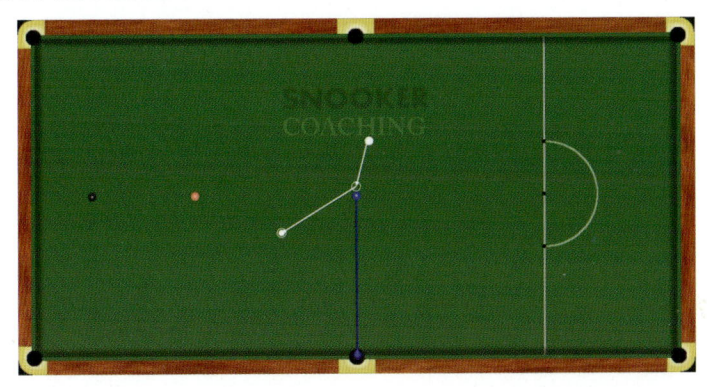

The Fifth shot – a 3/4 ball pot on Pink and stunning into position for the Black ball.

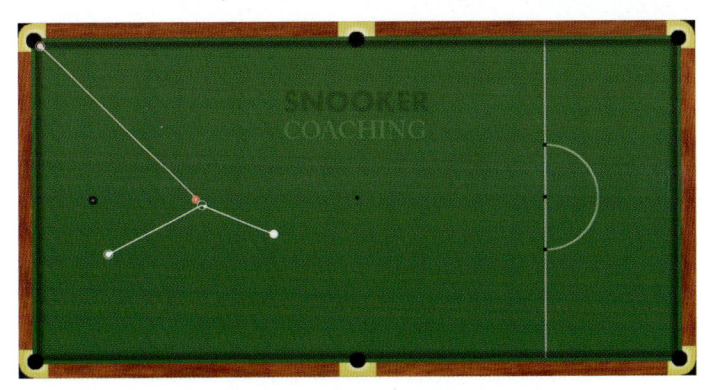

Pot Green

Pot the Green from the position illustrated.

Play slowly, bringing the Cue ball off the side cushion for position on Brown. This is not the best way as playing slowly across the nap can drift off, but one to know.

Complete 10 times.

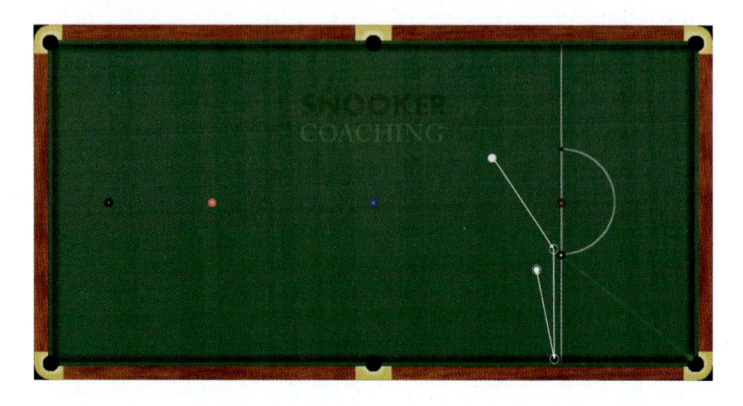

Also, complete 10 times but playing a little harder and sending the Cue ball across the table. Again, this is not necessarily the best shot to take on but one you should know. Play this a little harder to come off the side cushion and across the table for position on the Brown ball.

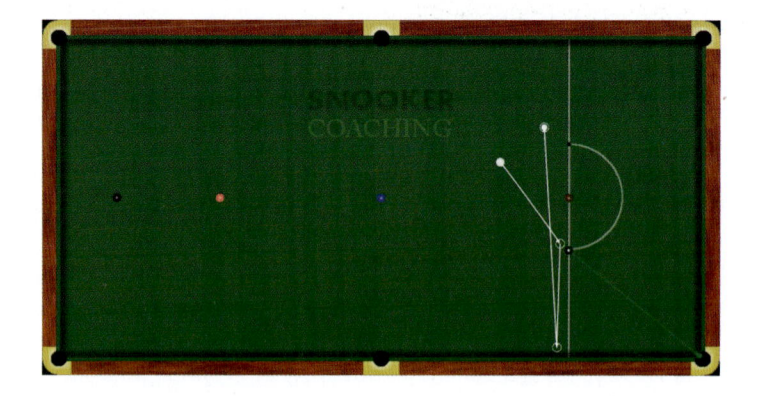

Also, complete 10 times but playing even stronger to come off both side cushions.

Again, not the best way to play the shot but another to know. Play harder still, coming off both side cushions for position on Brown.

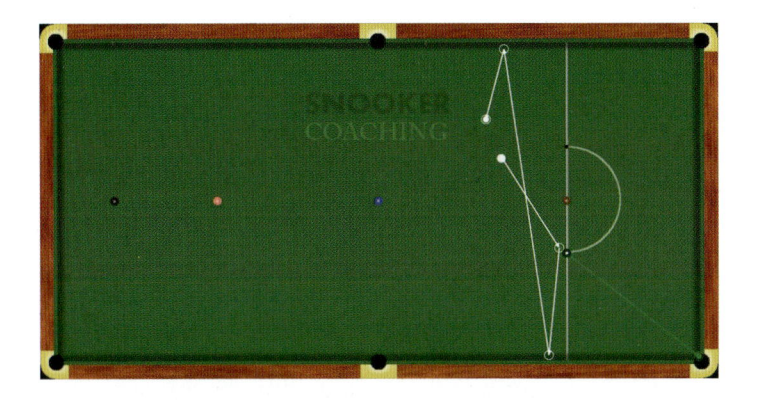

Also, complete 10 times but stun off the cushion for position on Brown. This is the best and most reliable way to play this shot, and the stun shot is medium paced to give a good position on the Brown ball.

A Final Clearance

Start with a 3/4 ball pot to middle pocket to gain an almost straight position on the Green ball.

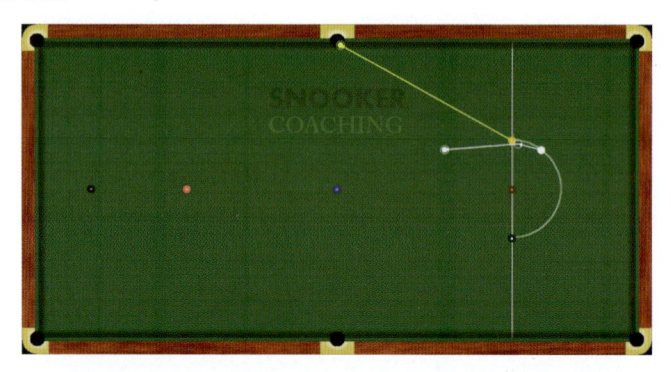

Easy pot on Green, screwing for position to leave a 3/4 ball pot on Brown.

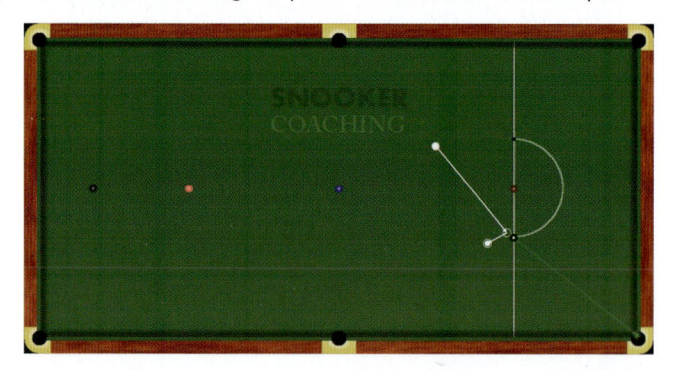

Pot Brown with a screw shot to gain position for a 3/4 ball pot on Blue. The rest is easy with a stun shot on the Pink ball for an easy position to pot the Black ball.

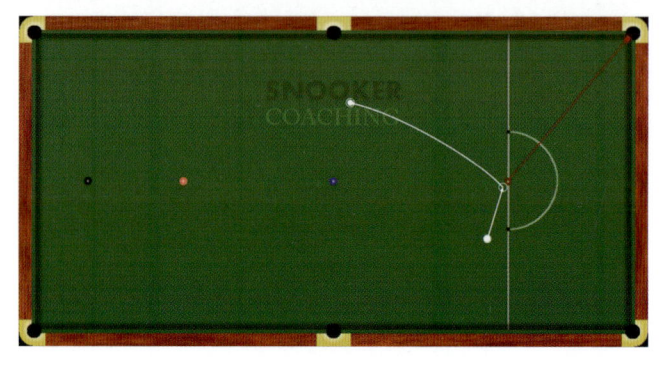

The Blue, Pink and Black should be plain sailing, so don't miss them!

Half-Ball Potting

From the exact position illustrated, complete 10 half-ball pots on Green, Brown, Blue, Pink and Black.

Useful shots to know, as sometimes from these positions it's very hard to see the exact point on the object ball that you need to hit. Knowing these half-ball pots gives you a point of reference.

Half-ball pot on Green.

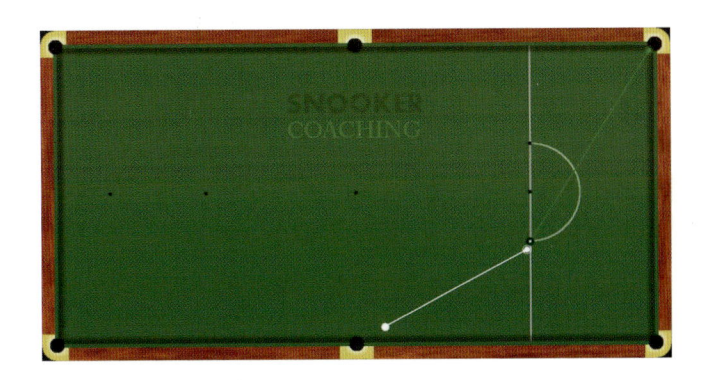

From about 7 inches from the baulk–line, recognize a half-ball pot on the Yellow ball.

With the White ball about the position illustrated along the side cushion, recognize a half-ball pot on the Brown ball to the middle pocket.

From the position illustrated, recognize a half-ball pot on the Blue ball to the middle pocket.

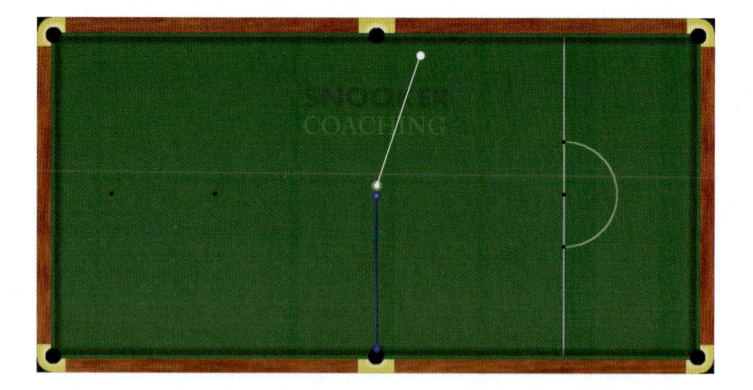

From about the position illustrated, recognize a half-ball pot on the Pink ball to the top pocket.

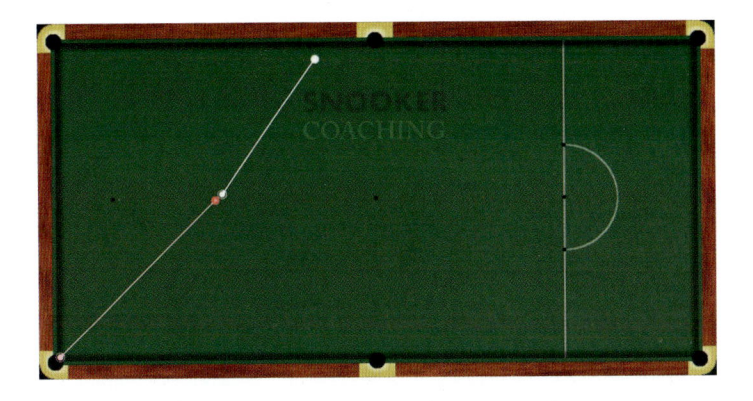

From about half-way between the Black and Pink spots, recognize a half-ball pot to the middle pocket.

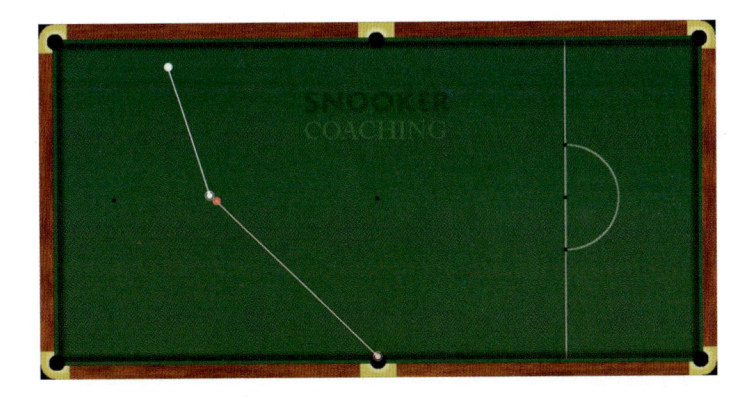

From about the position illustrated, recognize a half-ball pot on the Black ball to the top pocket.

Developing Touch

Nearly every player has tried this exercise, which goes back many years.

Place a ball tight against the cushion and in a position anywhere on the table that's easy for you to reach. Place the Cue ball 3 or 4 inches away from the ball on the cushion. Play little kiss shots, aiming to send the Cue ball back within the 3- or 4-inch distance.

This is a great exercise to develop touch and to ensure you don't grip the Cue too tightly.

Pot Blue and Split the Pack

Practise this exercise screwing into the Pink but also stunning into the Pink. Aim to make full-ball contact with the Pink.

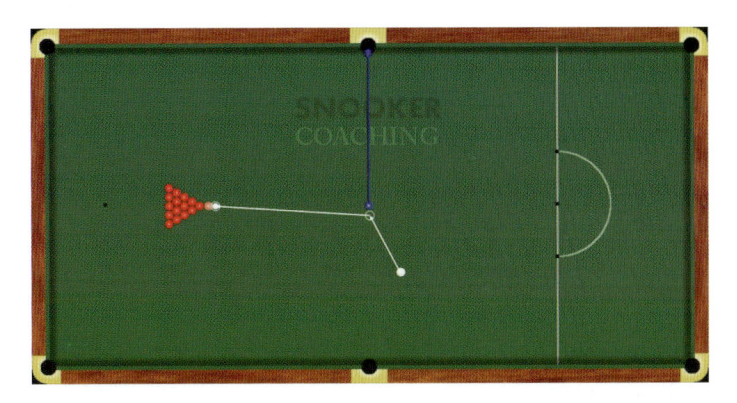

The Break-Off

From the position illustrated, aim to send the Cue ball onto the position marked on the bottom cushion.

Complete 10 times, ensuring that on each occasion you are no more than 3 inches away from your target. Important, because if you leave a loose Red, it could be the end of the frame!

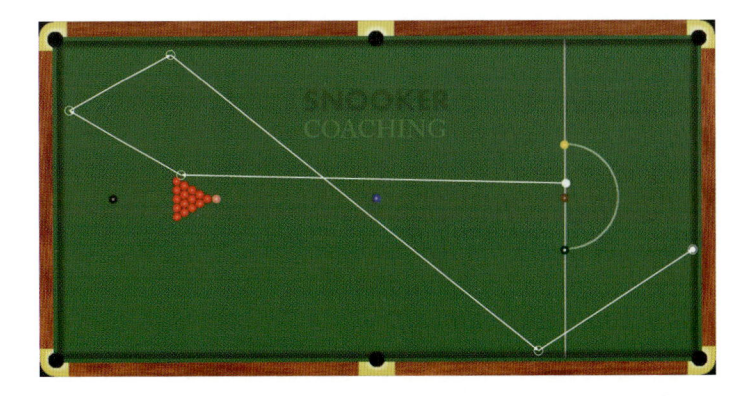

A Long Pot

Set the balls as illustrated.
    These sorts of opportunities may well be the only ones you get in a professional match, so don't miss – you will not get another chance!

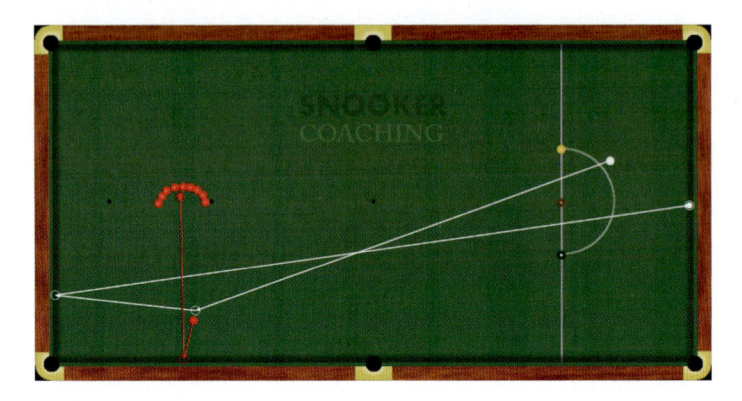

Cross Red Safety

Set the balls as illustrated.
    Complete three safety shots into the position indicated in baulk and with the Red ball into the semi-circle.

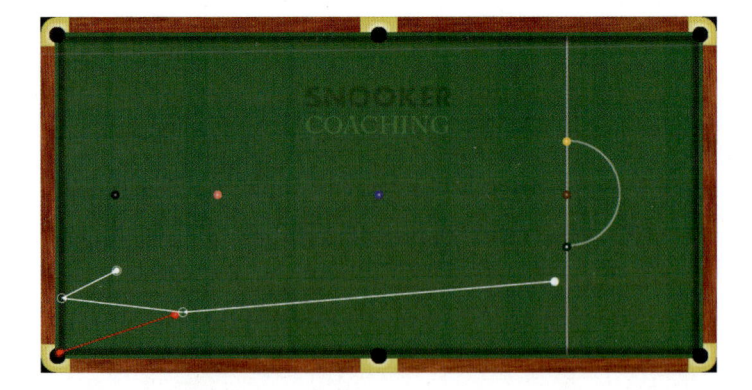

A Shot to Nothing

Set the balls as illustrated.
   Complete three safety shots into the position indicated in baulk – also try to make the pot on the Red.

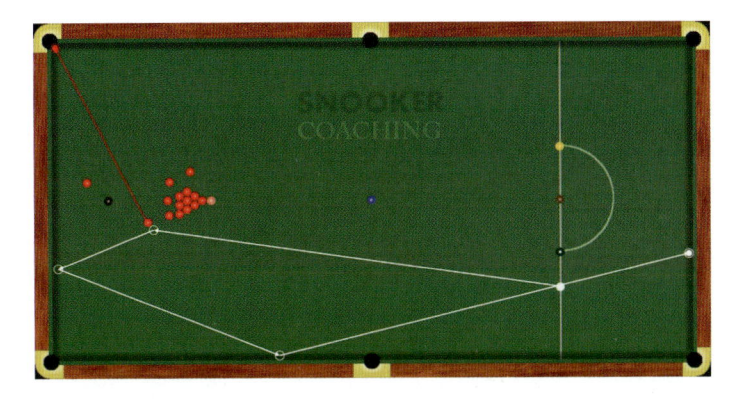

Yellow into Pack

Set the balls as illustrated.
   Aim to pot the Yellow and do so using screw and just a trace of left-hand side, which will draw the Cue ball into the pack. Quite an easy shot once mastered, but always remember the priority is the pot.
   You have practised this shot, so as well as the split try to make a break!

Safety into the Reds

Set the balls as illustrated.

Aim to drop the Cue ball gently into the line of reds.

Play until you can just contact the line of Reds without leaving any Reds on to pot.

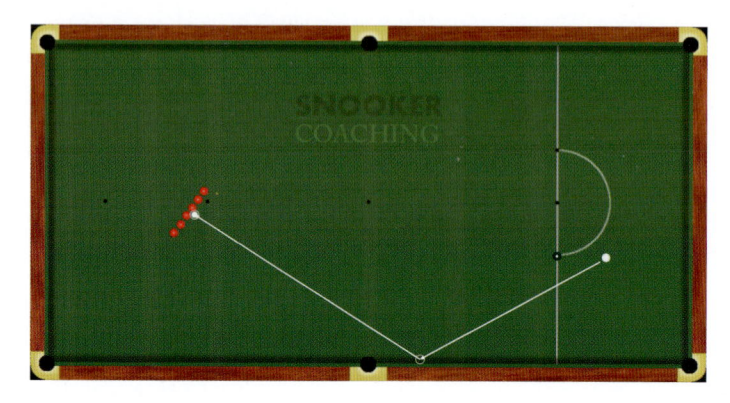

Blue Close Green

Set balls as illustrated.

This is a useful position to remember as you will just miss the Green to come up the table if it's close to a half-ball shot.

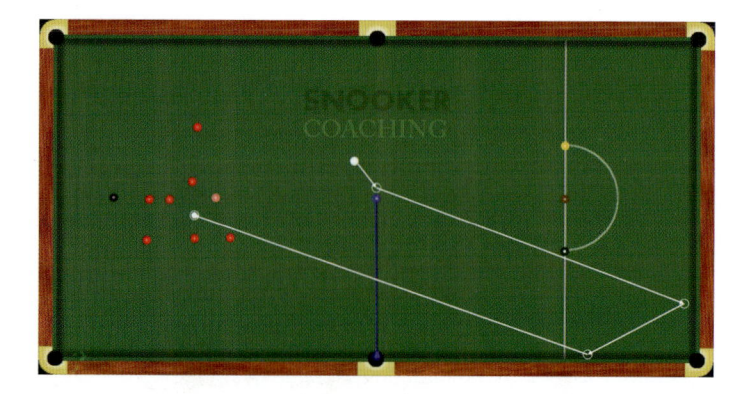

Swerve and Pot

Set balls as illustrated.
    Playing with left-hand side and slightly raising the butt of the Cue, aim to swerve round the obstacle and pot the Yellow. Continue with the same shot until you can pot the Yellow ball every time.

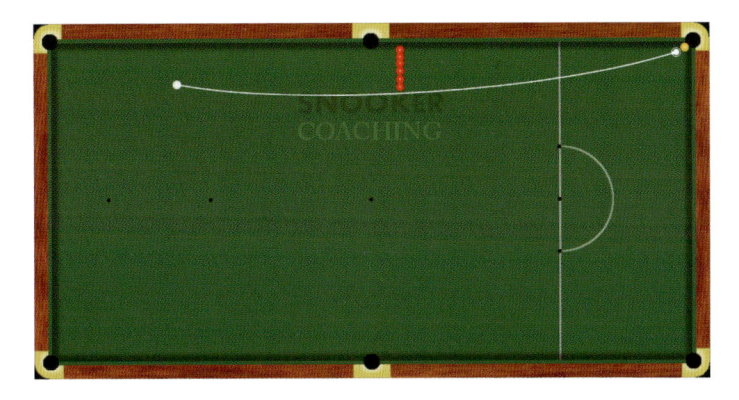

Safety Shot

Set the balls as illustrated.
    Aim to get the Cue ball into baulk as illustrated. This is a natural angle, so no side needed but be careful not to knock a Red ball onto another and into a potting position.

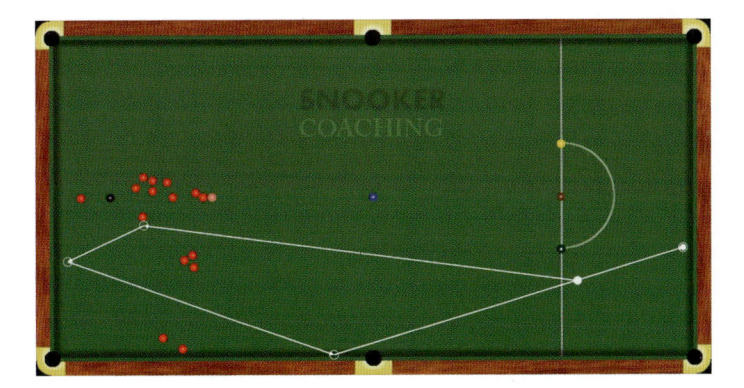

Safety Shot

Set the balls as illustrated.
 Aim to get the Cue ball into baulk as illustrated. This is a natural angle, so no side needed and aim to get the Cue ball as close to the bottom cushion as possible.

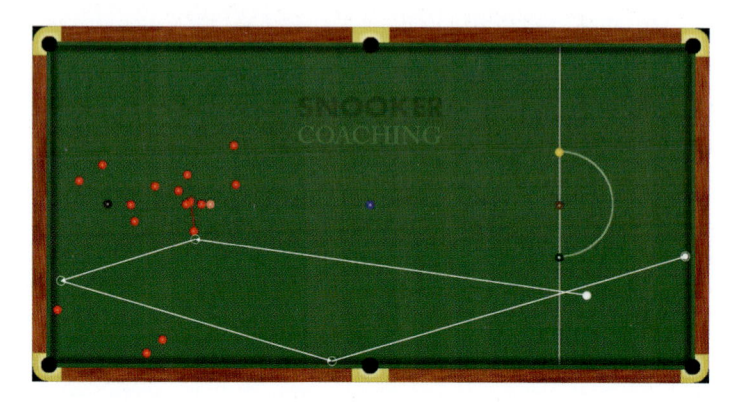

Safety Shot

Set the balls as illustrated.
 Aim to get the Cue ball into baulk as illustrated. This shot requires a trace of right-hand side and aim to get the Cue ball as close to the bottom cushion as possible.

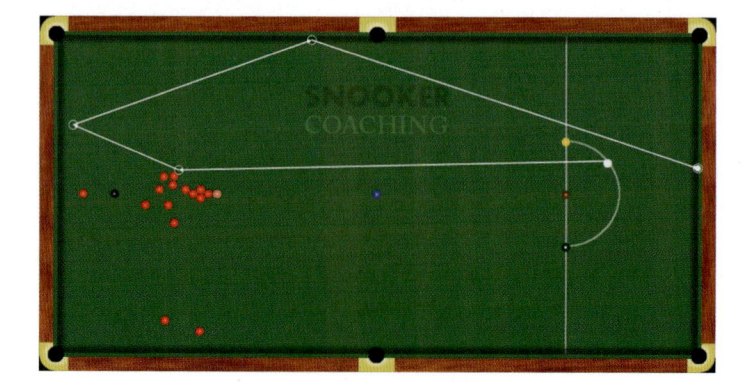

Safety Shot

Set the balls as illustrated.
　Aim to get the Cue ball into baulk as illustrated. This shot requires a screw, and aim to get the Cue ball as close to the bottom cushion as possible.

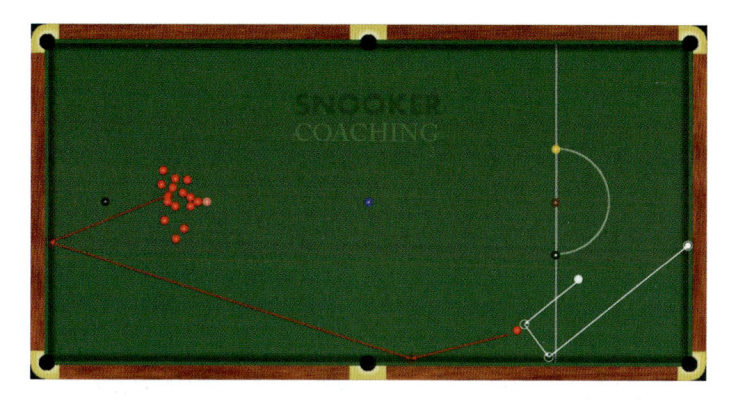

Shots to Nothing

Set the balls as illustrated.
　Use the natural angle to aim to pot the Red while coming off two cushions and back to be safe or to pot a baulk colour.

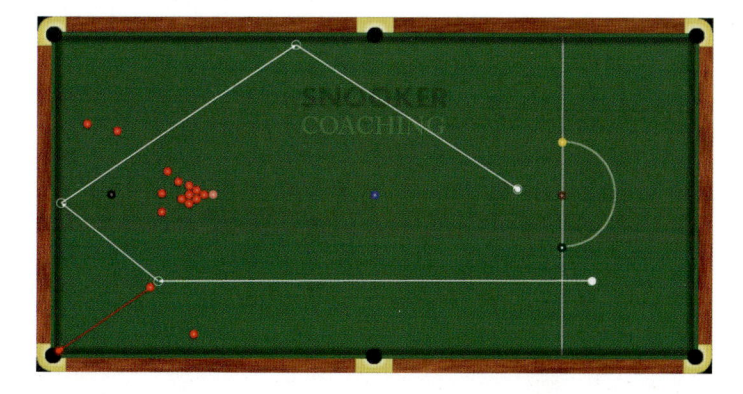

Shots to Nothing

Set the balls as illustrated.
 Use the natural angle to aim to pot the Red while coming off two cushions and back to baulk.

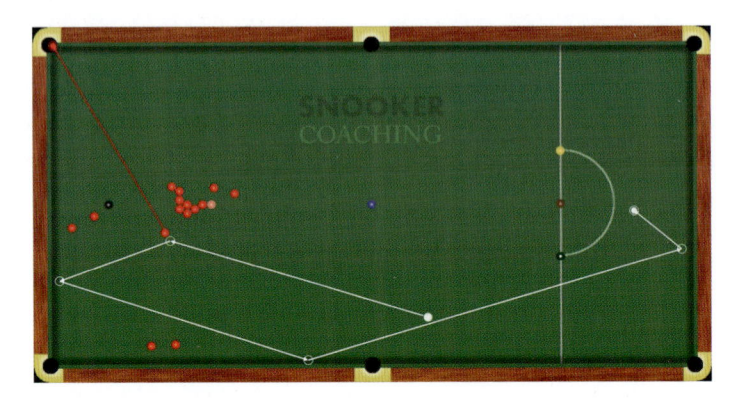

Shots to Nothing

Set the balls as illustrated.
 Using a gentle stun shot, aim to pot Red into middle, gaining position on Black but leaving nothing should you miss.

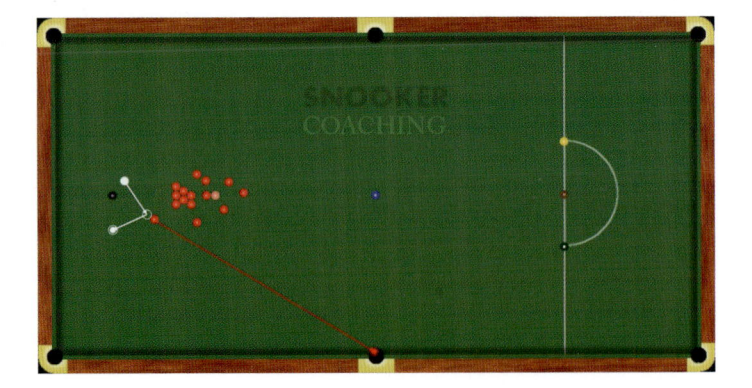

Shots to Nothing

Set the balls as illustrated.
   Using screw and right-hand side come off three cushions to return to baulk.

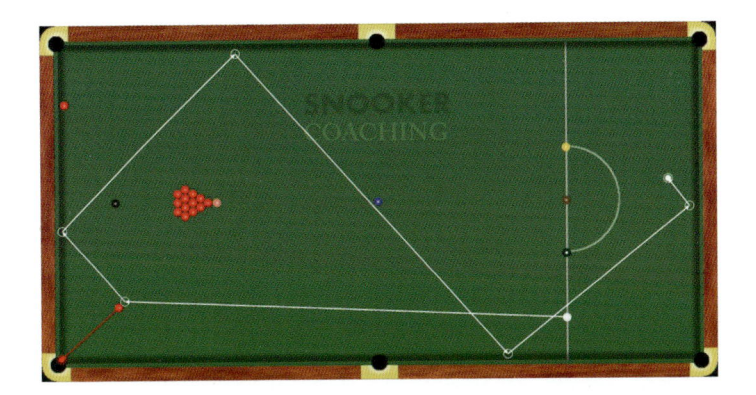

From this position just use the natural angle, and the Cue ball will return down the table. From here you can play a tight safety shot or leave a pot on the easy Blue to the middle.

Pot Blue and Split the Pack

Aim to hit the Pink full in the face and practise both screwing and stunning into the Pink.

Having practised this in previous lessons, you should be proficient at the shot now, so aim for five full-ball contacts on Pink in succession.

Half-Ball Safety off the Red

Aim to play a half-ball shot off the Red to snooker opponent behind Yellow.

This shot can gain you a better safety position than just a thin shot off the Red.

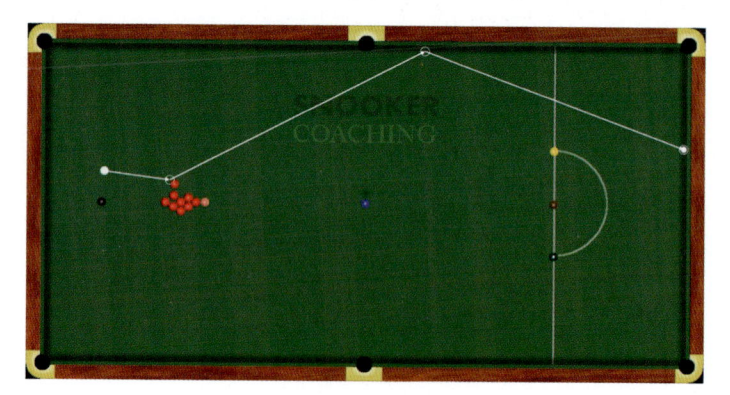

Safety off A Tempting Red

Although tempting, this shot provides a great opportunity to put your opponent in a difficult position. Opt for the safety shot and win the frame rather than risking losing the frame by taking on a low percentage shot.

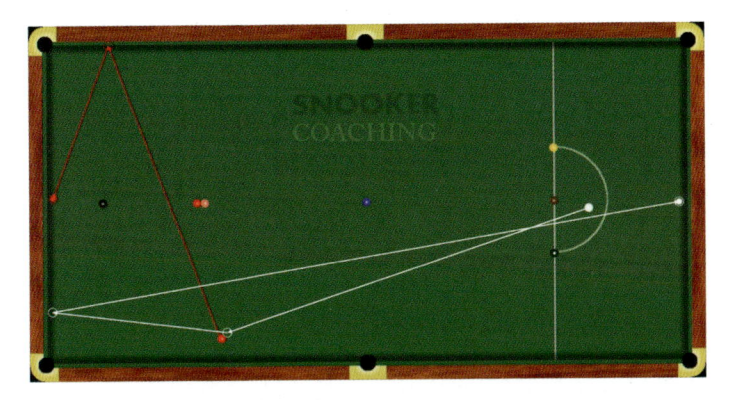

Pot Blue and Pink

From just off straight, pot Blue and run through a few inches to pot Pink. As with the previous exercise, this is keeping your concentration over a long period of play.

Pot Blue and Pink

From slightly further down the table, pot Blue using check side to gain position on Pink.

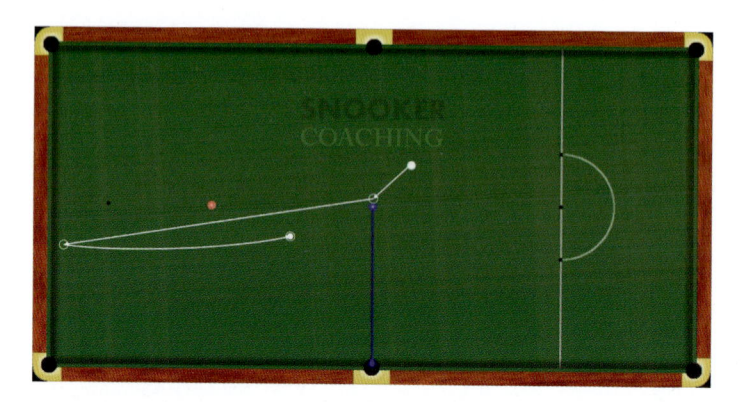

Safety off Green

Set the balls as illustrated.
   Aim to get the Cue ball behind the Black and the Green behind Brown.

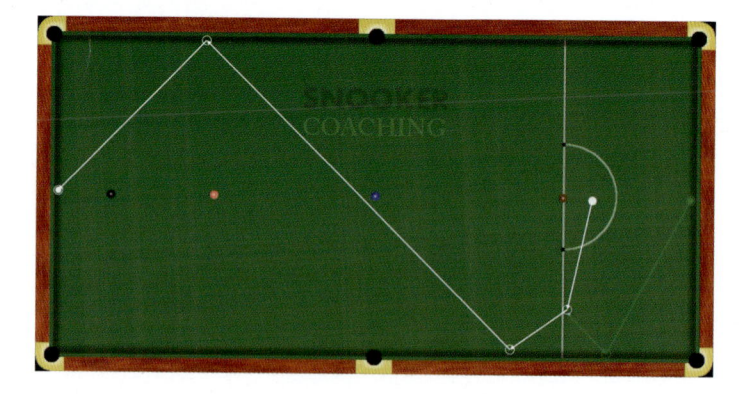

Safety off Blue

Set the balls as illustrated.
 Aim to get the Cue ball behind the Black and the Blue into the middle of the table.

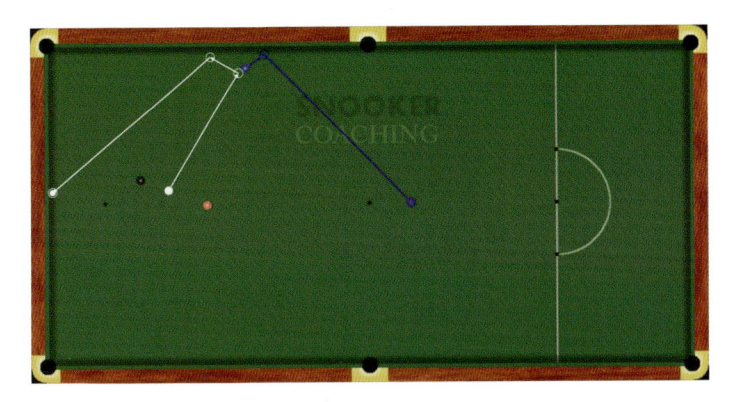

Safety off Pink

Set the balls as illustrated.
 Aim to get the Pink ball behind the Black by hitting a 3/4 ball with check side, which will bring the Cue ball back to baulk.

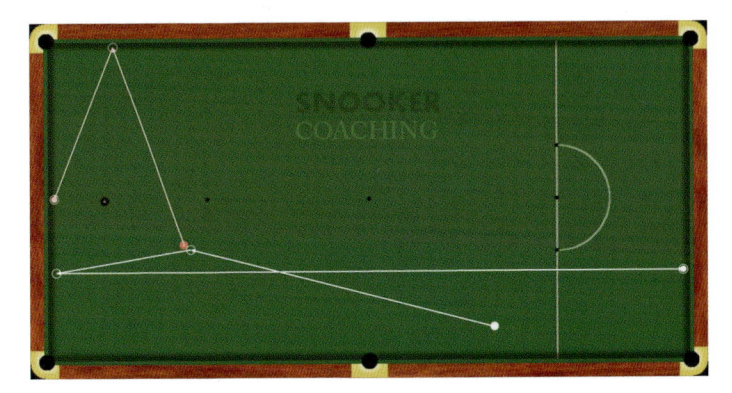

Snooker off Green

Set the balls as illustrated.
Aim to get the Cue ball behind the Brown and the Green behind the Pink.

Off-Straight Pink

Pot the slightly off-straight Pink then run off the cushion for position on the Black ball, which you must pot. Very easy – just concentrate!

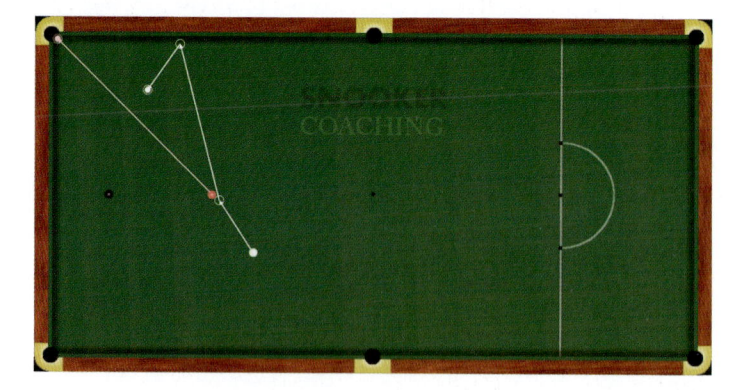

Pink and Run

Pot the Pink ball then run through for Black, which you must then pot to complete the set.
   Complete 10 sets of Pinks and Blacks in succession.
   Spend about 10 minutes on this exercise.

Nearside Pink

Pot Pink and run through to the nearside of Black, which you must then pot to complete the set.

Rest Work

With the rest, pot the Pink five times into each top pocket gaining position to pot Black.

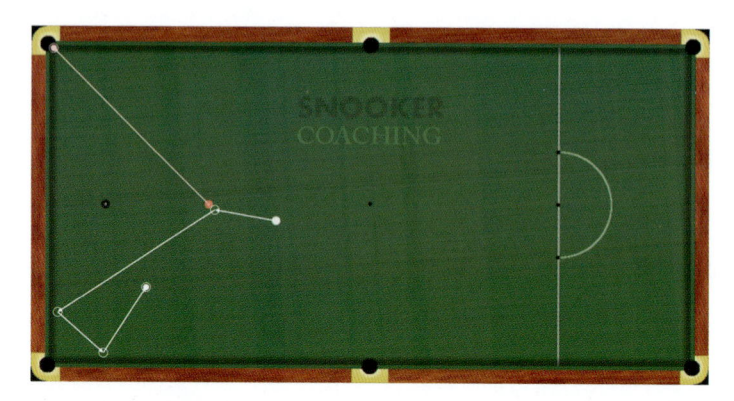

Pot Red and Blue

Set the balls as illustrated.
 Using a trace of side, pot the Red and screw off the side cushion for position on Blue. Having gained a great position, aim to make as high a break as possible.

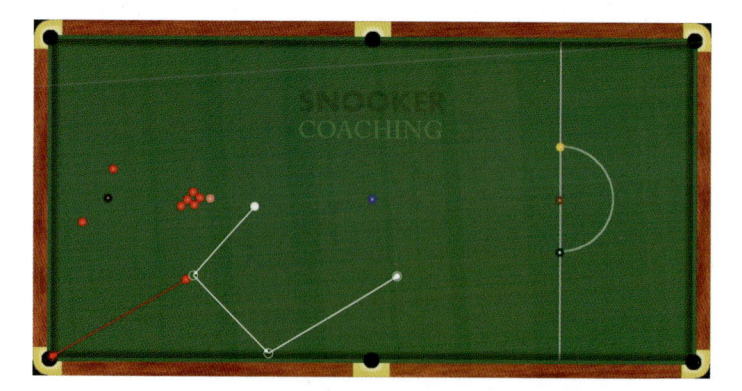

Stun off Brown

Set the balls as illustrated.
　Using a stun and a trace of side, aim to come off the bottom and side cushion to gain position on the Red. Aim to clear the table from the position you have gained.

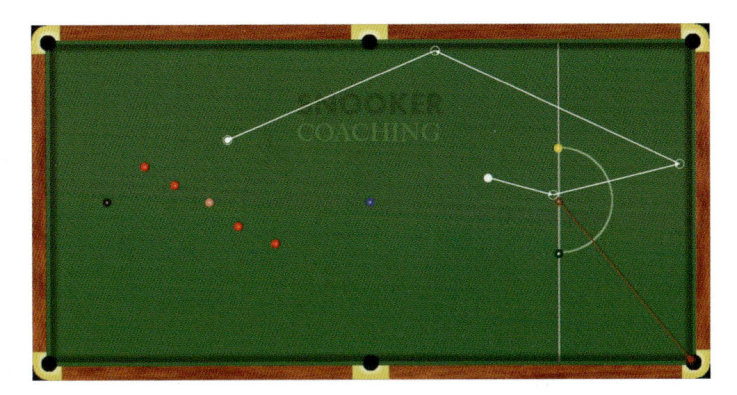

Run through Green

Set the balls as illustrated.
　Using top-spin, aim to pot Green and run off the bottom cushion to gain position on Red. Clear the table.
　In a match situation, this would be seen as a great opportunity, so try not to miss!

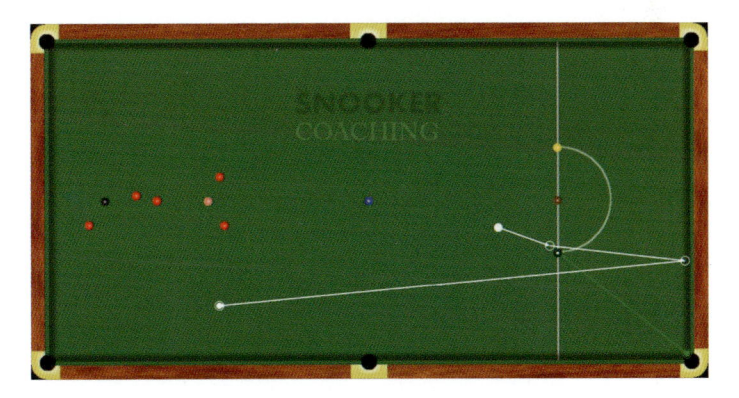

Screw off Yellow

Set the balls as illustrated.
  Aim to play a screw shot off Yellow to gain position on Blue. Pot Blue and clear the colours.
  Like the previous exercise, this one in a match would be a frame-winning opportunity, so try not to miss.

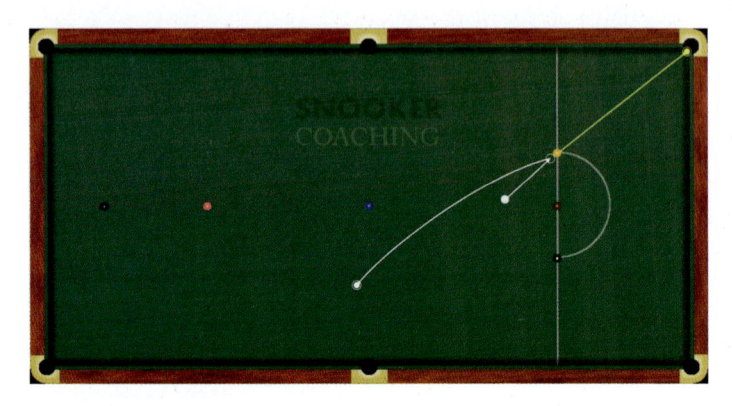

Screw off Cushion

Set the balls as illustrated.
  This is a 3/4 ball pot so requires the use of the cushion to gain position on Red. Pot Green and gain position on Red. Pot Red and aim to clear the table.

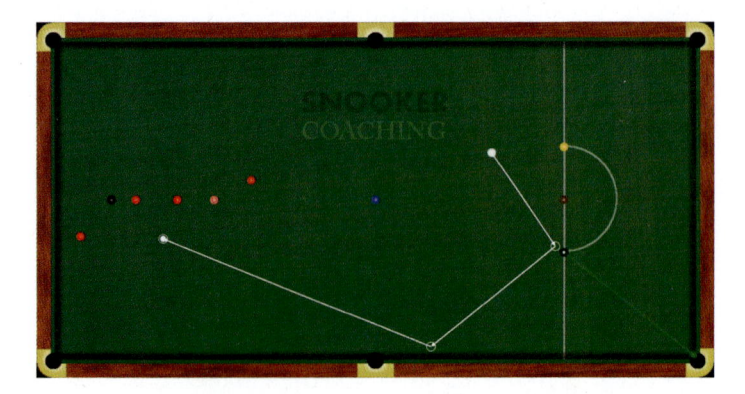

Escape 1

Set the balls as illustrated.
　Complete five escapes ensuring you strike the ball firmly enough so that if you miss it, the Cue ball is well away from the Red.
　A good point of reference when escaping from this sort of situation is to calculate a point halfway between the White ball and the Object ball, and if you hit this point you should contact the Object ball.

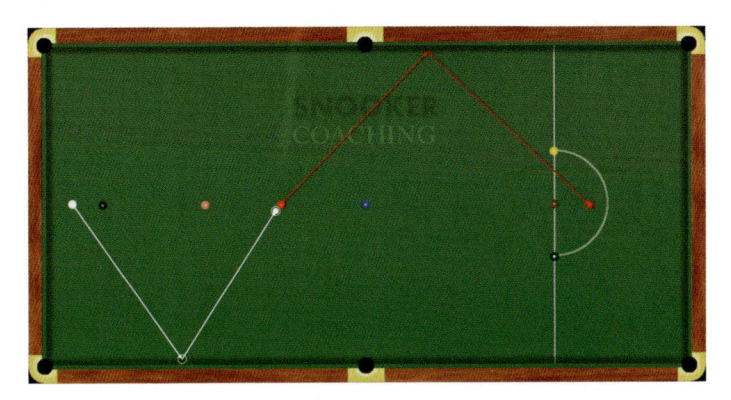

Escape 2

Set the balls as illustrated.
　Complete five escapes in succession, just resting dead weight on the isolated Red. Easy shot once you have established your line.

Escape 3

Set the balls as illustrated.
 Complete five escapes in succession aiming just to rest against the Reds without disturbing them. This one is very easy, so don't miss!

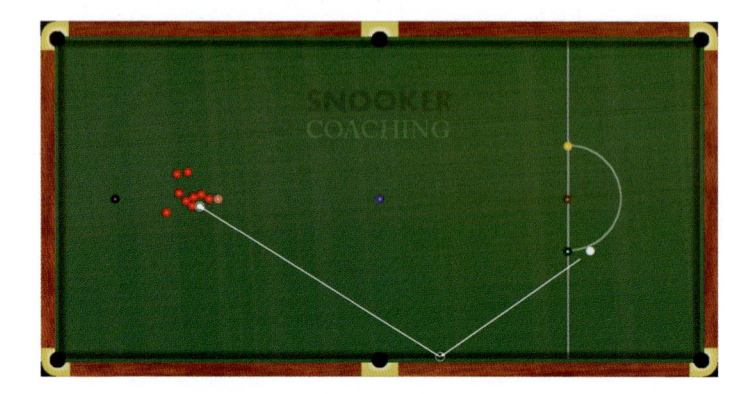

Escape 4

Set the balls as illustrated.
 Complete five escapes aiming to play with running side as the middle pocket is obscuring the natural angle. Don't hit the White ball too hard or you will find it almost impossible to be consistent in a shot like this.

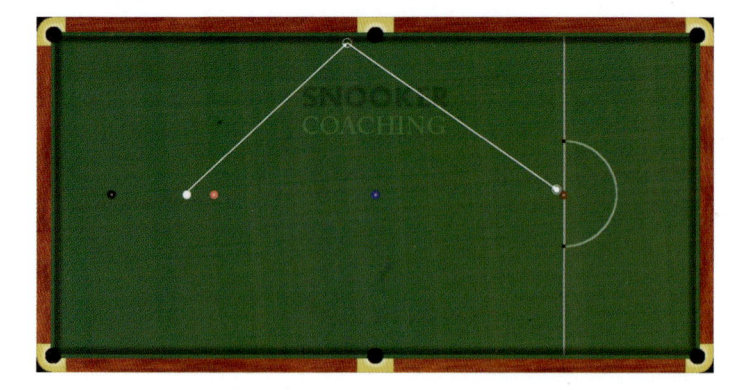

Cocked Hat Shot

Set balls as illustrated.
  One as old as the game itself but still can have its uses, so get to know the angles coming off three cushions.

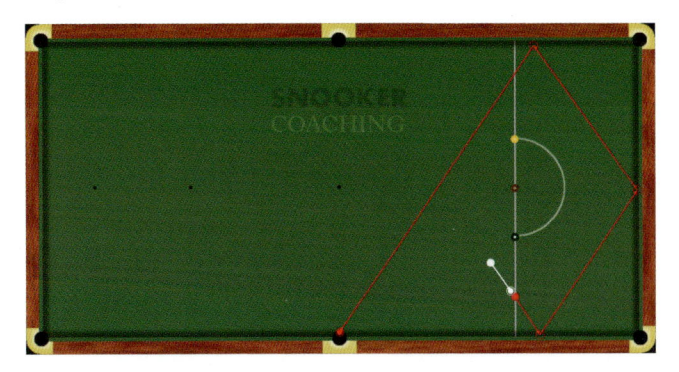

Cut-Back Doubles

Set balls as illustrated.
  Almost shots to nothing, as both these situations can be played knowing that the Cue ball should end up in a safe position.

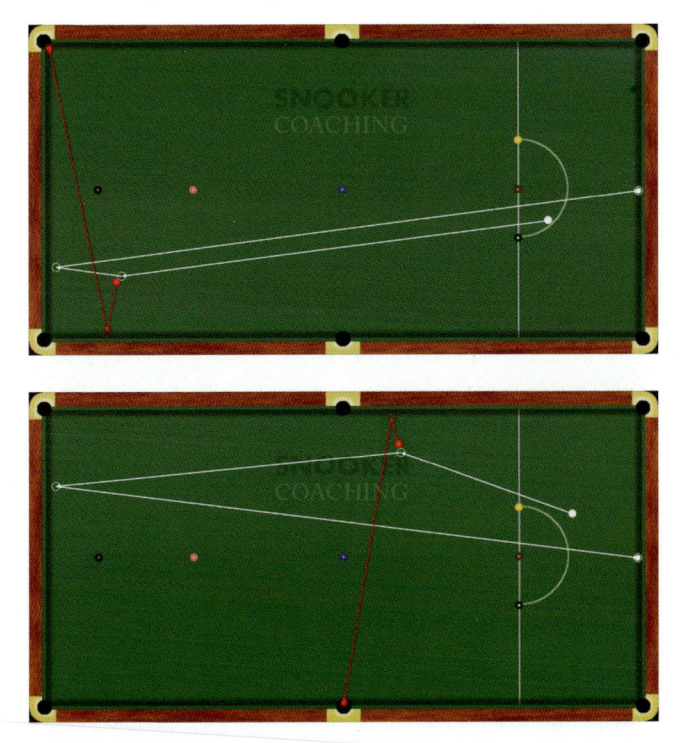

The Cross Double

Set balls as illustrated.

Complete the pot, but it only counts if the Cue ball ends up behind the baulk line.

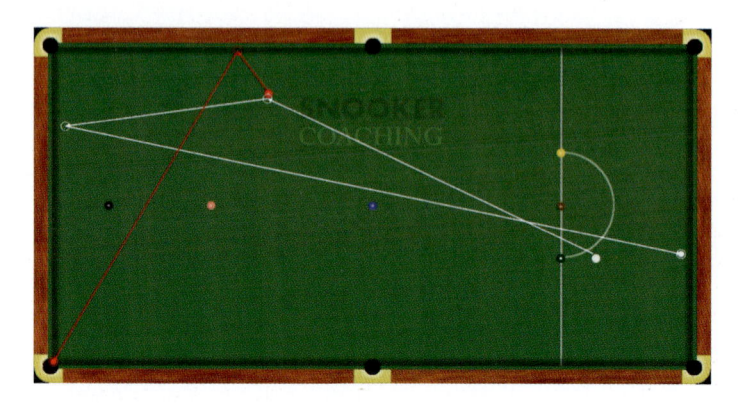

Roll-Up Escape

Set balls as illustrated.

This is a very gentle shot that you need to master so that you can escape from the snooker but leave the Cue ball and object ball so close that a pot is impossible.

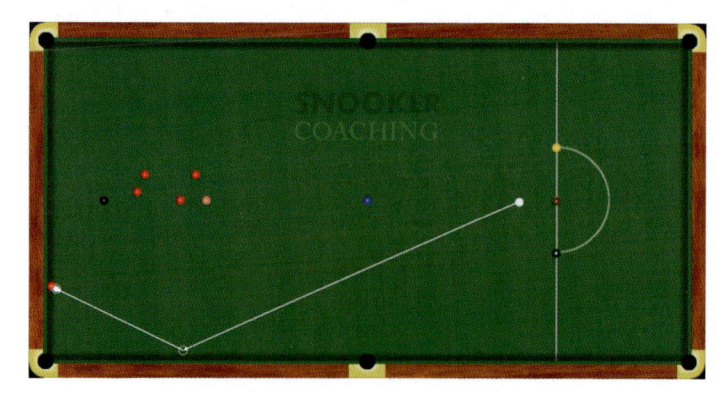

Roll Up to Red

Set balls as illustrated.
　A simple roll-up shot trying to get the Cue ball and object ball very close together.

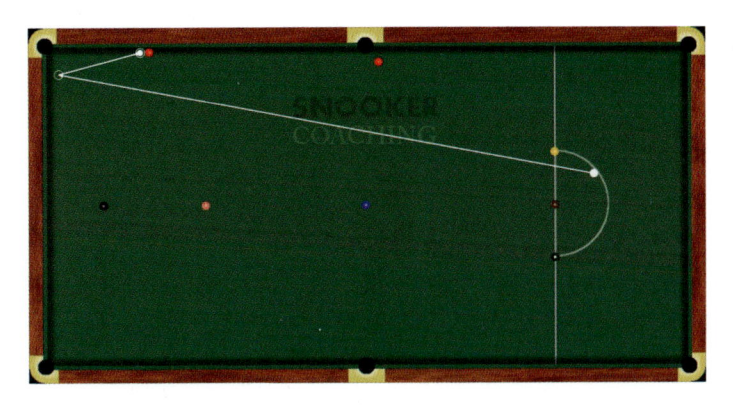

Ball and Cushion

Set balls as illustrated.
　Play ball and cushion together to pot Red and gain position to pot Black.

A Shot to Nothing

Set the balls as illustrated.
   Complete three pots, but they only count if you also manage to get the Cue ball behind the baulk line.

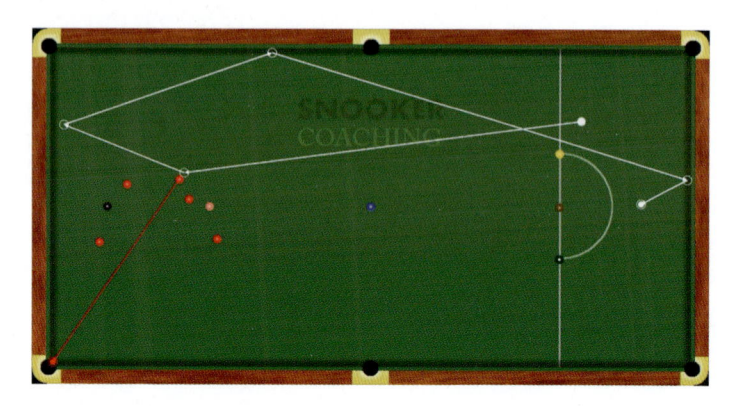

Snooker off the Red

Set the balls as illustrated.
   Complete three snookers by laying the Red behind the Black, Pink and Blue balls. Once you have completed this exercise, set the balls as illustrated in the second illustration.

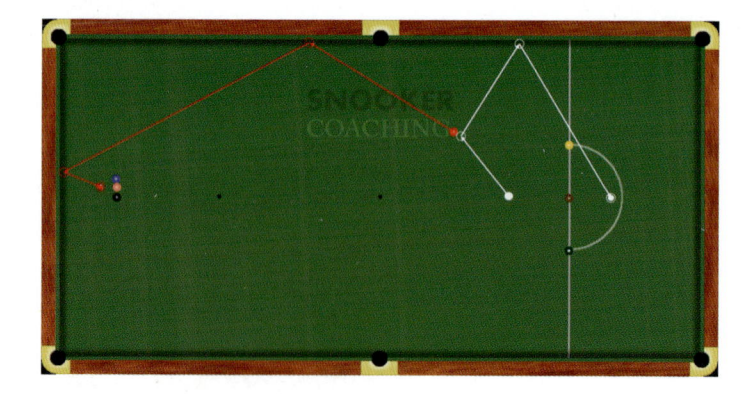

This time, play thin off the Yellow to place the Cue ball behind Black, Pink and Blue Balls and the Yellow behind the line of Reds. Complete five times.

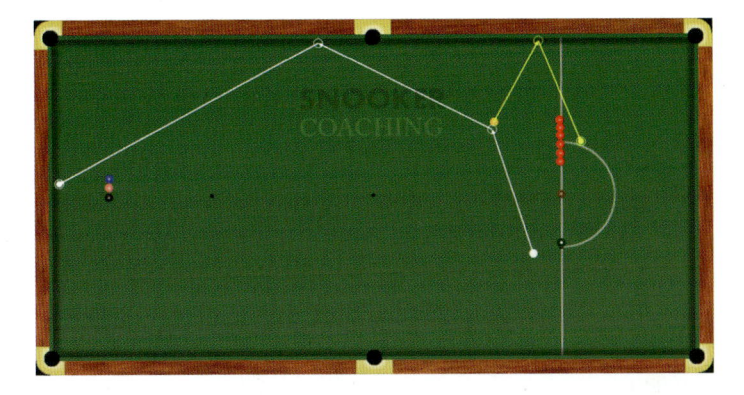

This time, play thin off the Blue to place the Cue ball behind Pink and Black. Complete five times.

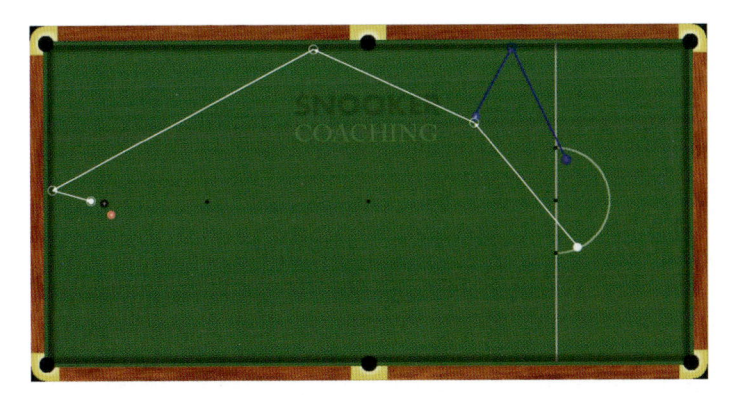

Safety off Black

Set the balls as illustrated.
　Play a 3/4 ball across the Black to leave the Cue ball at the top of the table and Black in baulk.
　Complete successfully 10 times in succession.

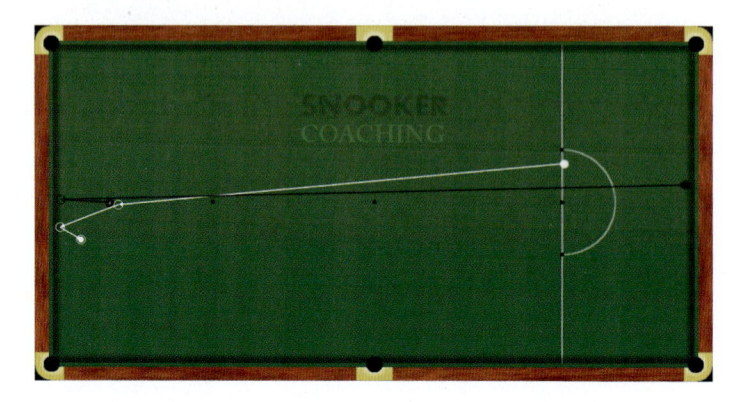

1/4 Ball Double

Set balls as illustrated.
　Not a shot you will use many times, however, one to know. Hit the Red ball with a 1/4 ball contact to double into the middle pocket.

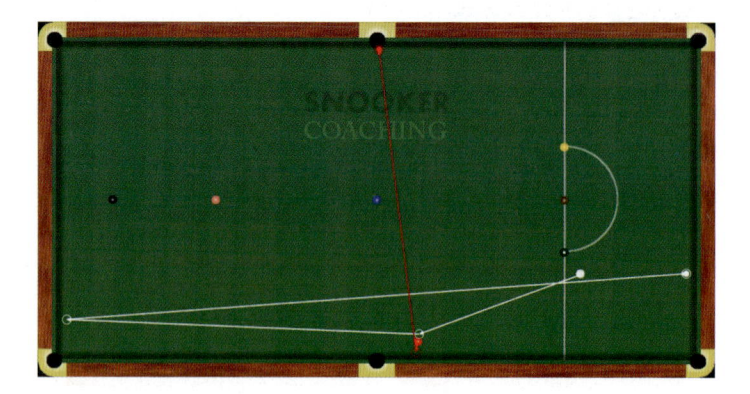

Cross Double

Set balls as illustrated.
　Amazing how many times this shot crops up in a match, so become proficient at it as you will need to play it.

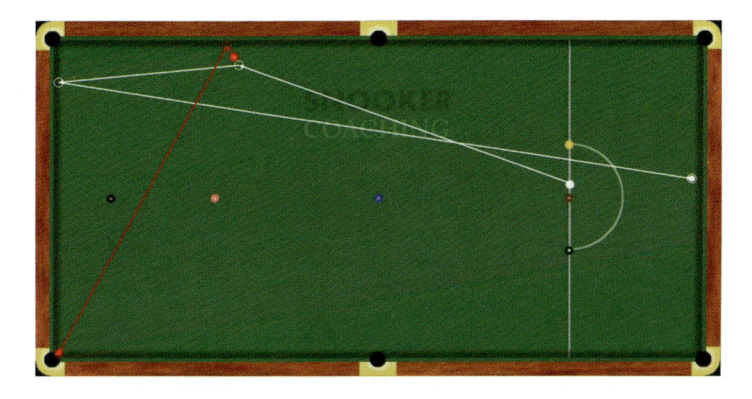

Double to Middle

Set the balls as illustrated.
　Aim to pot the Red into the middle by doubling off the top cushion. A useful shot as even if you miss the pot you should still have achieved a snooker on your opponent.

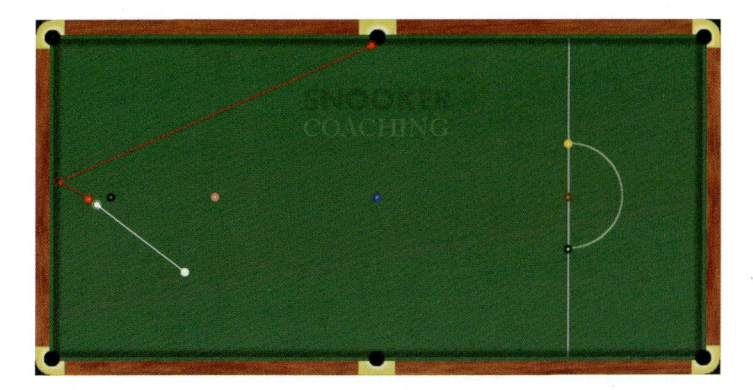

The Cocked Hat Double

Set the balls as illustrated.

You have practised this one before in exercises so should know how to play this shot.

Aim to pot the Red into the middle by doubling off three cushions.

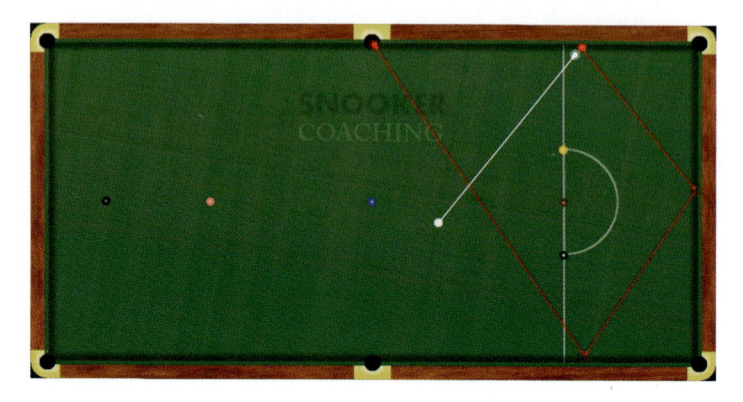

Pack Split

You have practised this exercise before, so now you must pot the Yellow ball and at least make some contact with the pack on every attempt at this exercise. Running side (left) required.

Split the pack off the Yellow 10 times and aim to make a break off the split.

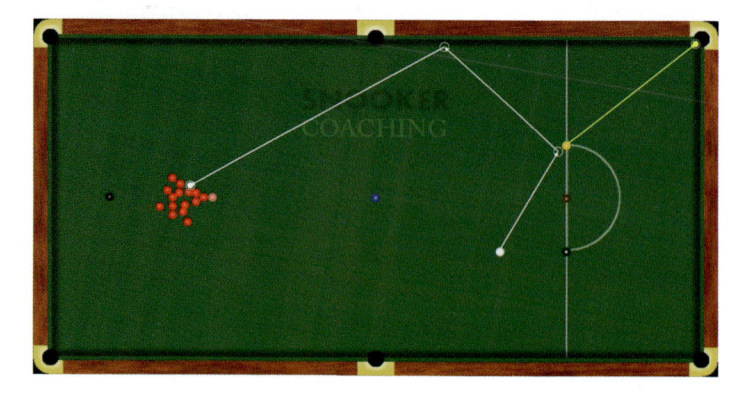

Green Split

Again, one that you will have practised in previous exercises, so you must at least make the pot and contact with the pack. Running side (right) needed here.
   Split the pack off the Green 10 times. Also, aim to make a break off the split.

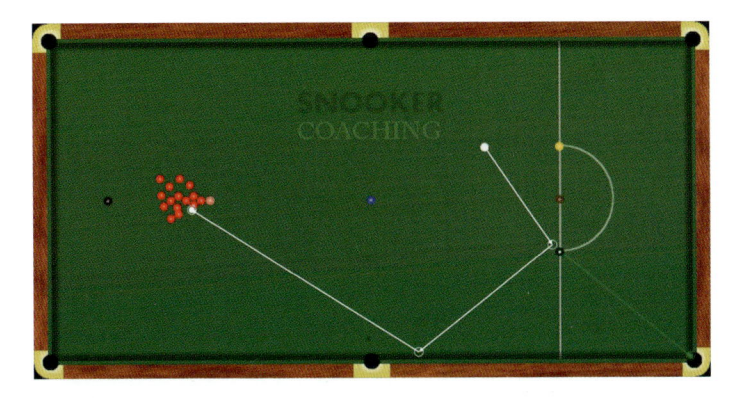

Blue Split

Using a screw shot aim to pot the Blue ball to middle and make full-ball contact on the Pink ball.
   Split the pack off the Blue 10 times and aim to make a break off the split.

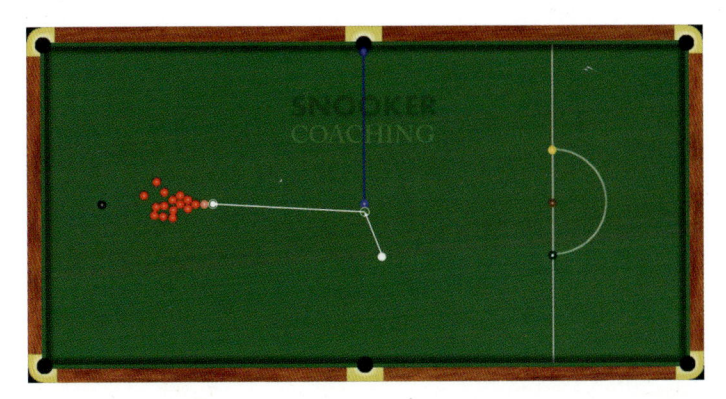

Split Pack 30

You should now be highly proficient at splitting the pack so now, and before you can move on from this stage, you must split the pack and make a 30+ break.

Split the pack off the Blue and score a 30+ break at least once, but for the better players five times.

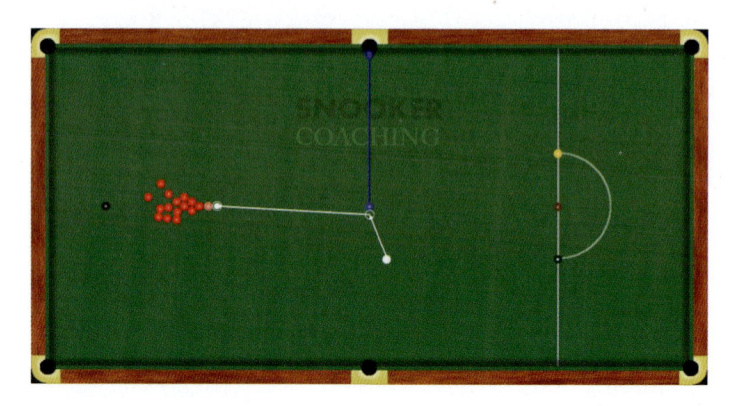

The Squeezed Set

Place the balls as indicated.

You will see that the sets are not in a direct line with the pocket; however, by striking the balls on the left-hand side of the picture on the right-hand side the set can be squeezed into the pocket.

The balls on the right-hand side of the table need to be struck on the left-hand side to squeeze the set into the pocket.

The T Set

Set the balls as illustrated. Given that the Reds are touching it becomes a natural set for the bottom pocket and the middle pocket.
Complete three times from each position and having completed the pot, continue and make a clearance.

Given that the Yellow and Blue balls are touching it becomes a natural set for the Blue ball to the middle pocket.

Easy Plant

An easy plant and a shot to nothing plant (second illustration).

Set the balls as illustrated.

Aim to make the easy plant (three times in succession) then also make the harder plant and send the Cue ball back into baulk.

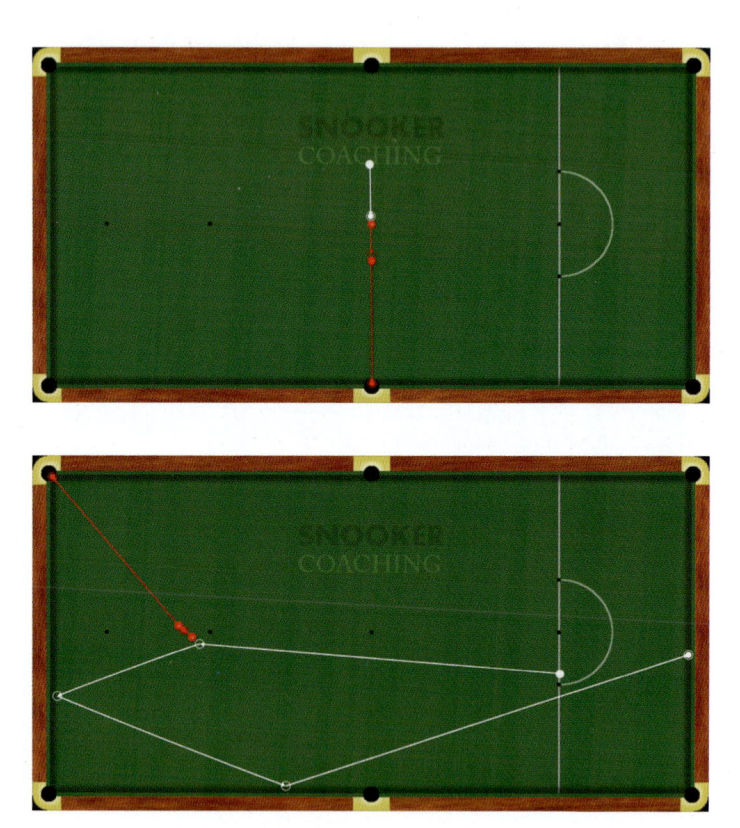

Blue from 3 Positions

Set the balls as illustrated.
From the first and almost straight position drop the Blue in striking at 12 o'clock to just roll into position for Pink. Don't miss, and clear the other colours.

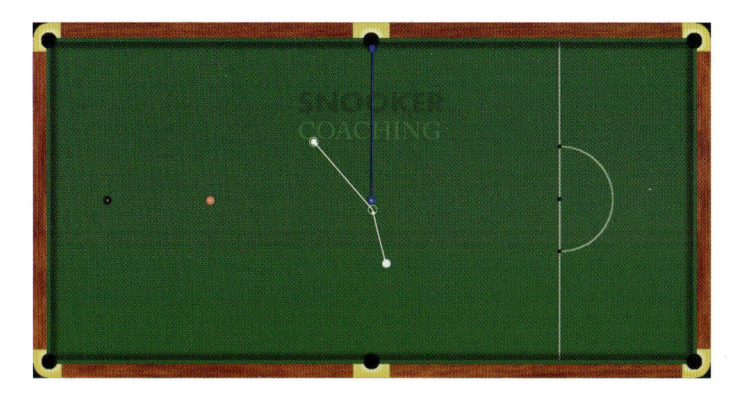

From position two again strike at 12 o'clock, and the Cue ball follows the natural angle for position on Pink. Clear Pink and Black after potting Blue.

From position three you need to strike the Cue ball at 10 o'clock, which imparts left-hand spin and checks the Cue ball off the top cushion for Pink. Also, clear Pink and Black.

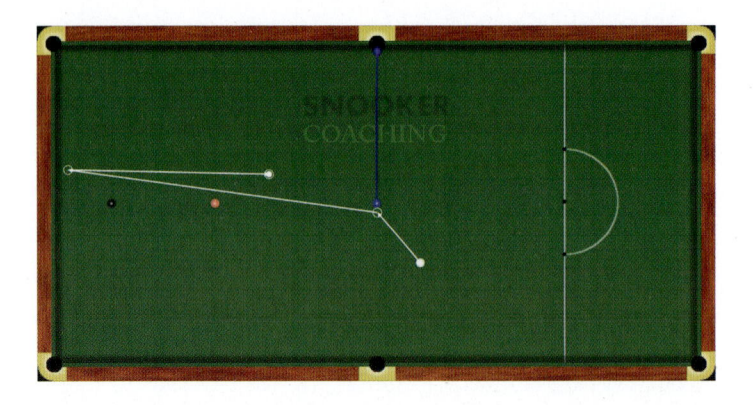

Also, practise the same shots from the other side of the table where the shots are the same apart from the third shot, which, instead of striking at 10 o'clock, you need to strike at 2 o'clock.

Complete three pots on Blue and three on Pink from each position, making a total of 36 pots.

Pink from 3 Positions

Set the balls as illustrated.

From position one pot Pink and stun the Cue ball for position on Black. Pot Black.

From position two hit the Cue ball at 12 o'clock to come off the side cushion gaining position for Black. Pot Black.

From position three you need to strike at 5 o'clock and with power to send the Cue ball off four cushions for position on Black. Pot Black.

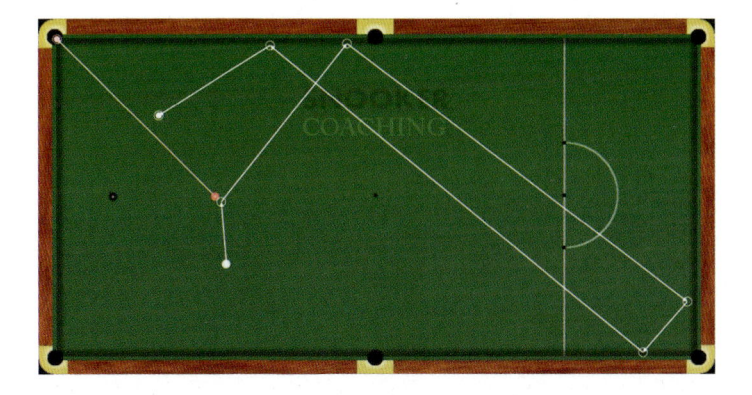

Repeat the above shots from the opposite side of the table, the only difference being that from the third position you strike the Cue ball at 7 o'clock, not 5 o'clock.

Stun to Pink

Set the balls as illustrated.
   Pot the Blue ball and stun into the Pink ball, ensuring you hit the Pink ball full in the face.

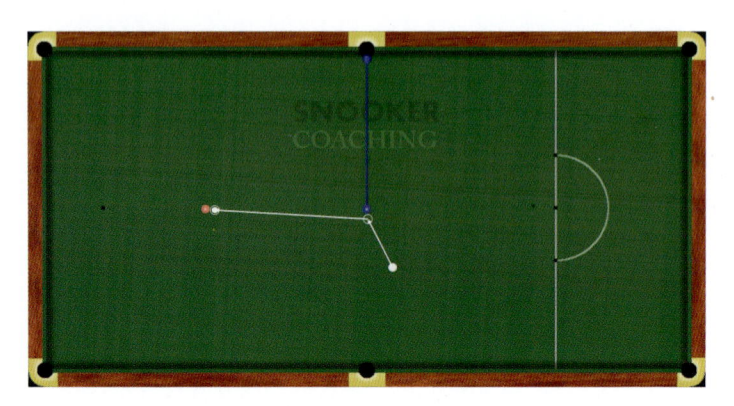

Screw to Pink

Set the balls as illustrated.
   Pot Blue but this time instead of a stun shot as with the previous exercise screw into the Pink ball hitting Pink full in the face.

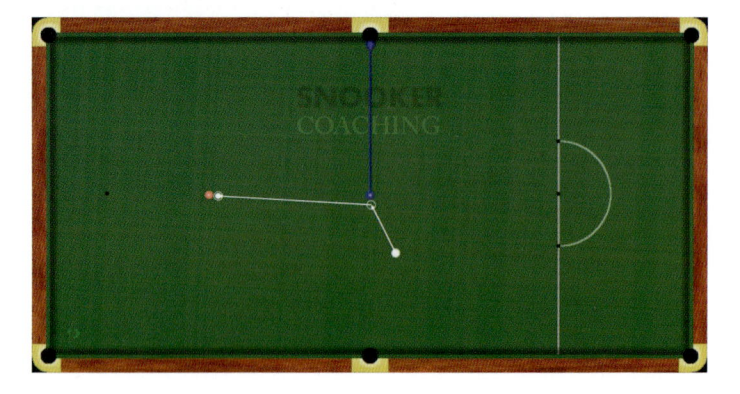

Pink to Middle From 3 Positions

Set the balls as illustrated.
   From position one, strike the Cue ball at 12 o'clock to gain position on Black. Complete the pot on Pink and Black three times.

From the second position pot Pink and stun into position on Black. Complete the pot on Pink and Black three times.

From the third position, play a simple screw shot for position on Black. Complete the pot on Pink and Black three times.

Practise from both sides of the table as the shots are the same, requiring no side to gain position on Black.

Practice on Black

A combination of shots on the Black aimed to get you really in practice and to increase consistency on the Black.

Pot Black, stunning off the top cushion for position on Black. Complete 30 pots and position from each pot.

Complete 30 pots from each side of the table (60 in total), using a gentle run through with no side.

Set the balls as illustrated.
Complete 30 pots from each side of the table (60 in total) using a top spin with no side.

A Useful Snooker Shot

Set the balls as illustrated.
　Play this shot as a stun shot without side. Red back to baulk and White behind the Black.

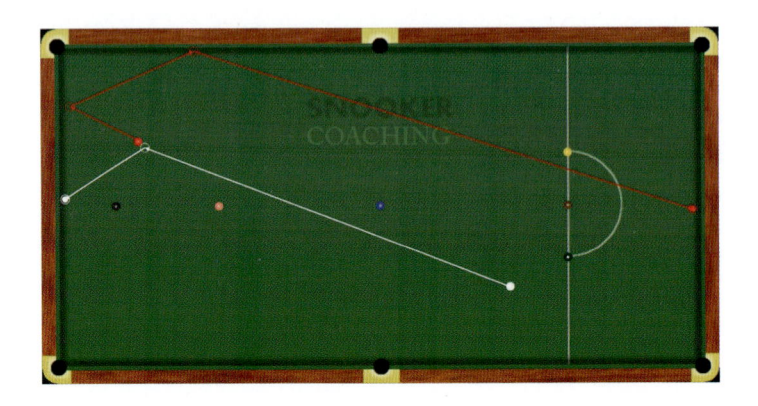

A Useful Snooker Shot

Set the balls as illustrated.
　Play this by striking the Cue ball dead centre with no side.

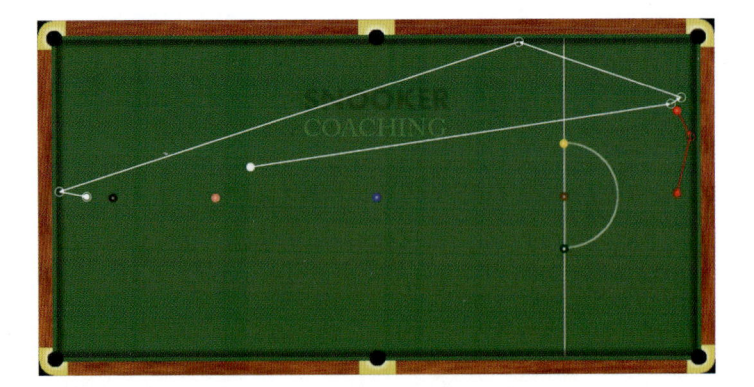

A Snooker Escape

Set the balls as illustrated.
   Play this by striking the Cue ball low, firm and with no side, which will help the Cue ball stay low as it strikes the first cushion.

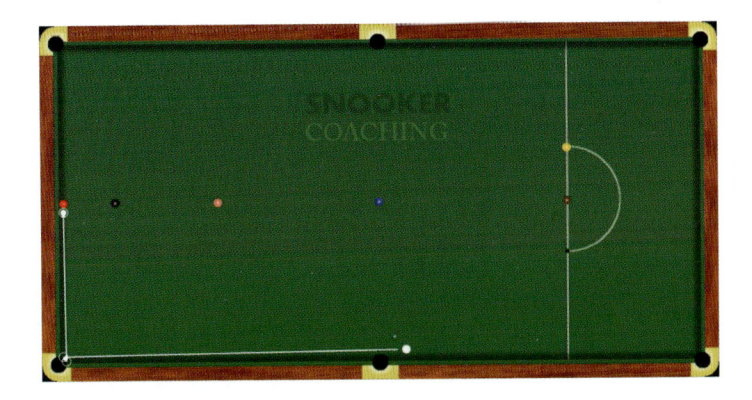

Two Cushion Split

Set the balls as illustrated.
   Using top and left-hand side swing the Cue ball into the pack off two cushions. You need to experiment a little to get the exact start position for the White ball, so it is fine to miss a few shots until you know where to start and how much side to apply.

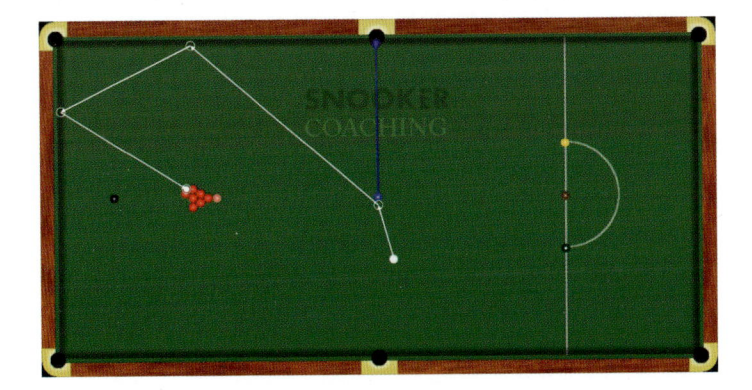

Wrong Side of Blue

Set the balls as illustrated.
　Use stun and right-hand side to go between Yellow and Brown then back down the table for position on a Red.
　Concentrate, as top players must be proficient at this sort of shot.

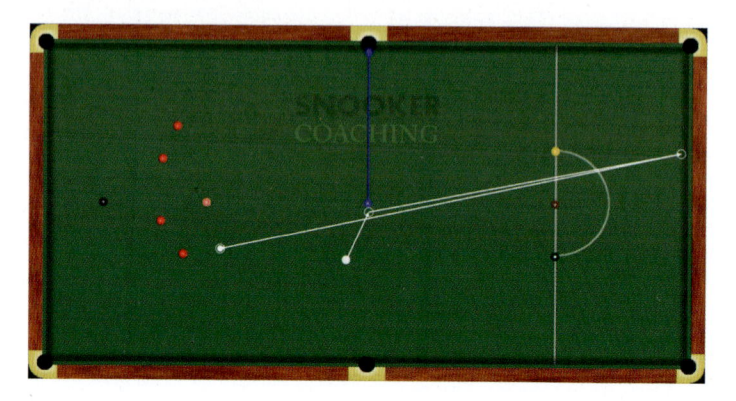

Running Left

Set the balls as illustrated.
　Use running left-hand side to go between Yellow and Brown and off two cushions for position on Red.
　Again, a shot you must master, so concentrate!

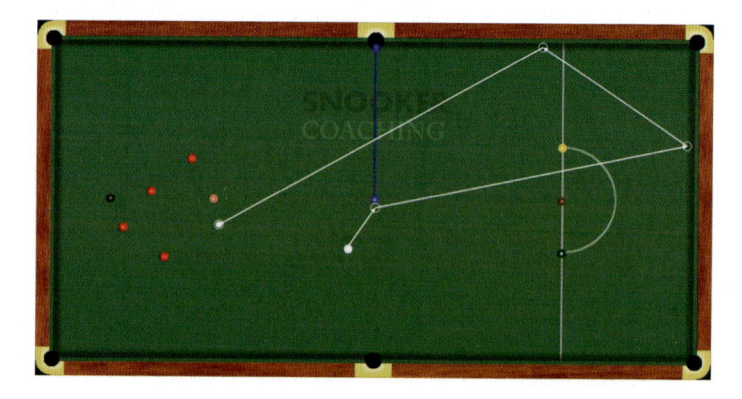

Screw and Right

Set the balls as illustrated.
　　Using screw and right-hand side go between the Brown and Green balls and off two cushions for position on a Red.

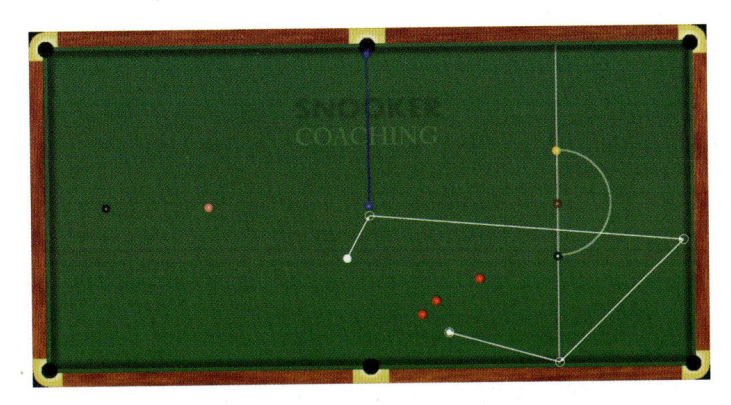

Black to Yellow

Set the balls as illustrated.
　　Pot Black, running off two cushions to gain position on Yellow.

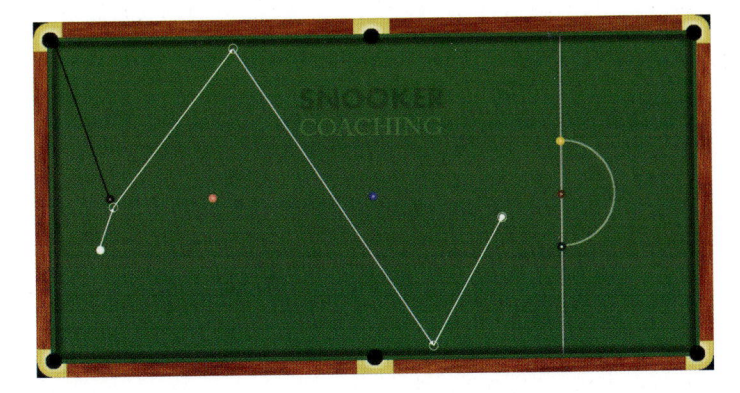

Black to Yellow

Set the balls as illustrated.
　Pot Black by screwing with left-hand side to come off the side cushion to gain position on Yellow.

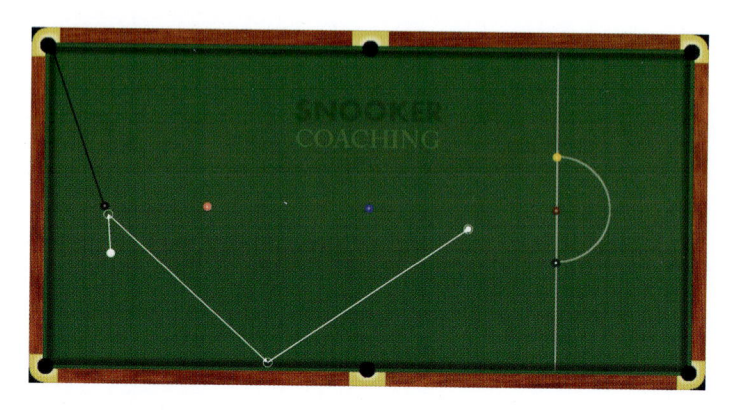

Black to Yellow

Set the balls as illustrated.
　Pot Black by screwing with right-hand side to gain position on Yellow.

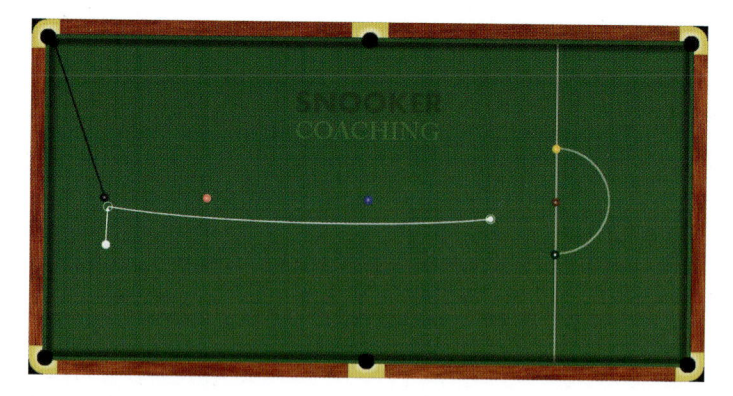

Half-Ball Black to Yellow

Set the balls as illustrated.
   Pot the half-ball Black with just a trace of left hand side to miss Pink and to gain position on Yellow.

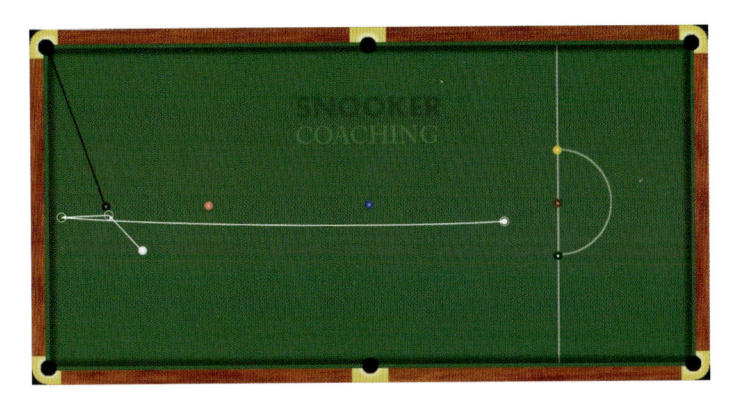

Stun and Side Black to Yellow

Set the balls as illustrated.
   Pot Black by using a stun shot with left-hand side to come off the top and side cushion to gain position on Yellow.

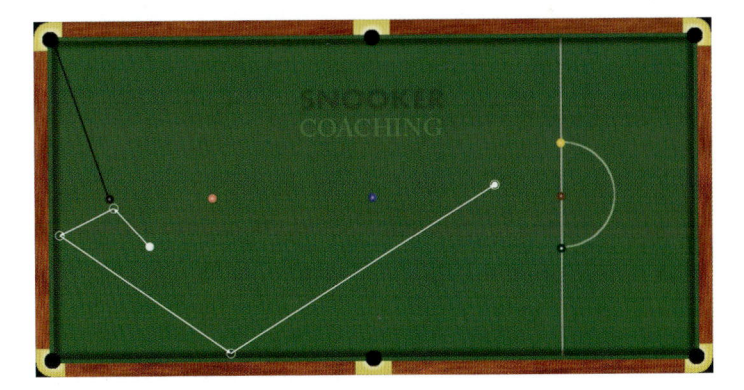

Straight on Black to Yellow

Set the balls as illustrated.
　Pot Black by screwing with strong left-hand side to come off the side cushion to gain position on Yellow.

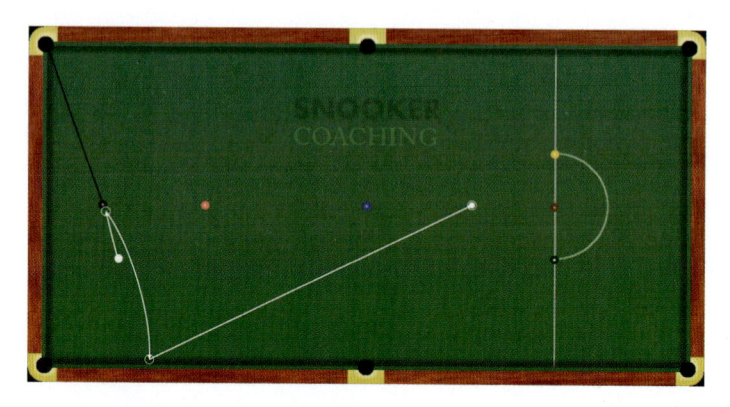

Stun to Yellow from Black

Set the balls as illustrated.
　Pot Black with a stun shot and no side to come off the side cushion to gain position on Yellow.

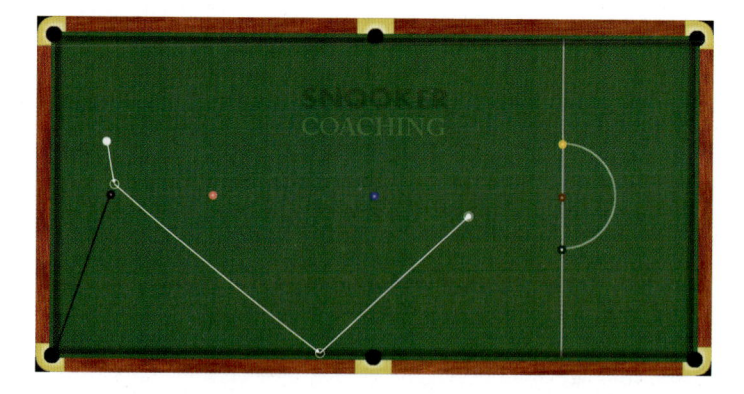

Pot Black Left-Hand Side for Yellow

Set the balls as illustrated.
   Pot Black coming off the top cushion to just miss Pink and gain position on Yellow. For this shot, you will need a trace of left-hand side to avoid contact on the Pink ball.

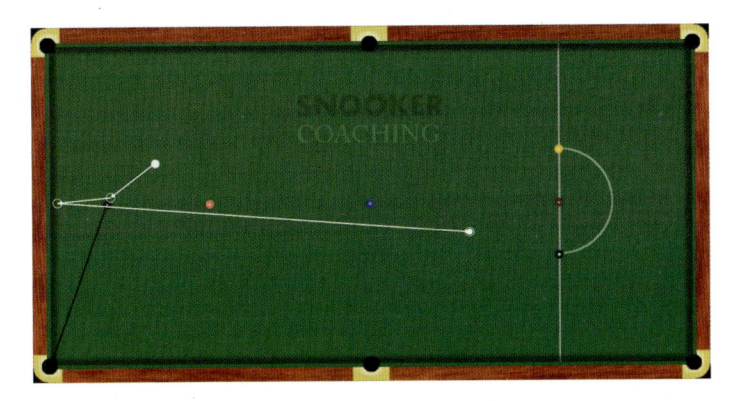

Almost Straight to Yellow

Set the balls as illustrated.
   Pot Black with a power shot and left-hand side to come off the top and the side cushion to gain position on Yellow.

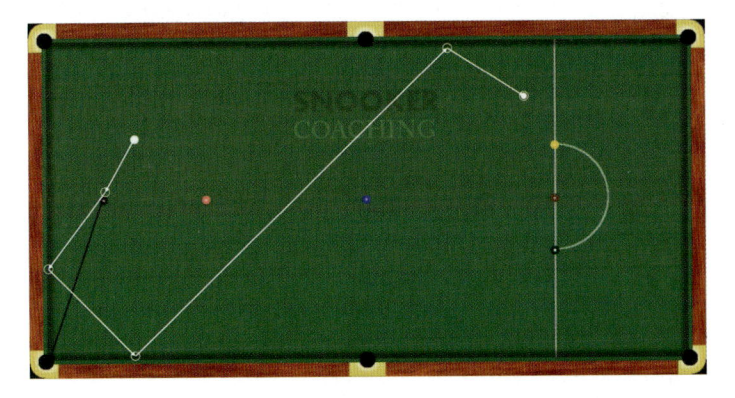

Wrong Side of Blue to Yellow

Set the balls as illustrated.
   Pot the Blue with top and left-hand side to gain position on Yellow.

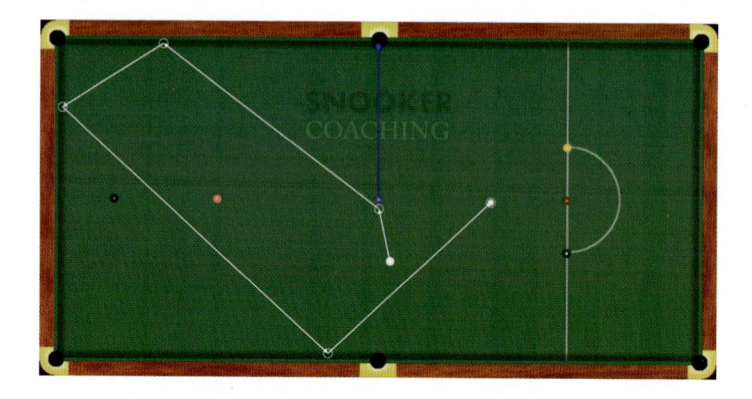

Wrong Side of Blue to Yellow

Set the balls as illustrated.
   Pot Blue with a little screw and left-hand side, coming off the top and side cushions to gain position on Yellow.

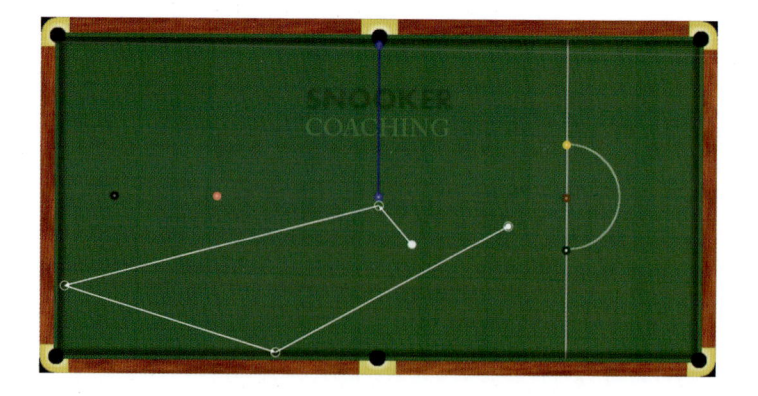

Wrong Side of Blue to Yellow

Set the balls as illustrated.
 Pot Blue with a stun and right-hand side, coming off the top and side cushions to gain position on Yellow.

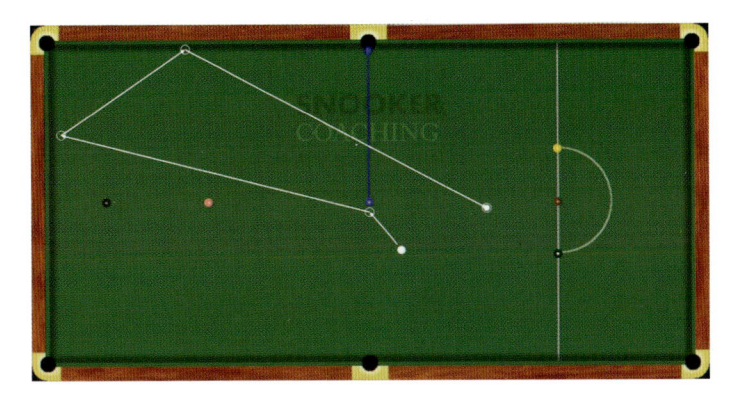

Pro Safety

Detailed in the illustrations below are 10 different situations to play safe from. Each of these situations has been taken from actual situations in professional matches. Starting from the first illustration set the balls as illustrated and complete satisfactorily each safety shot three times before moving on to the second situation.
 First Shot – thin off the Red ball into baulk and the Red ball covered by the Pink ball.

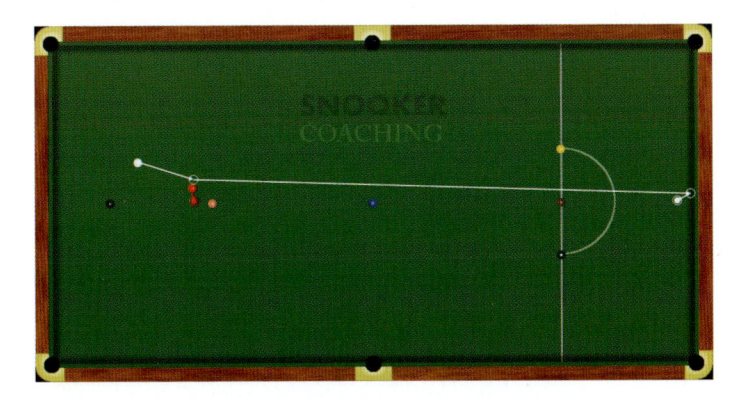

Second Shot – thin off the Yellow, sending the Yellow behind Brown and the White behind Black.

Spend 5 minutes on this exercise.

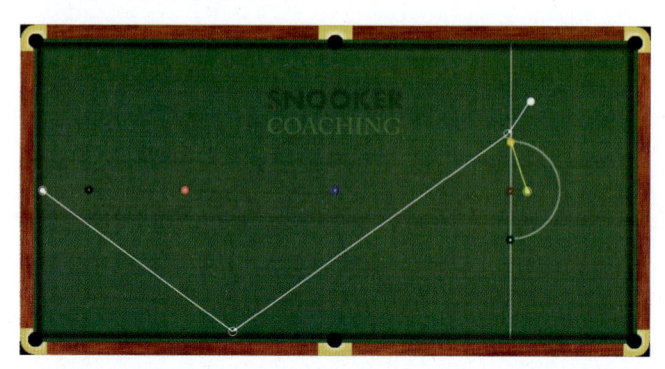

Third Shot – from the Yellow spot send the White off three cushions and back to baulk and send the Black to the side cushion.

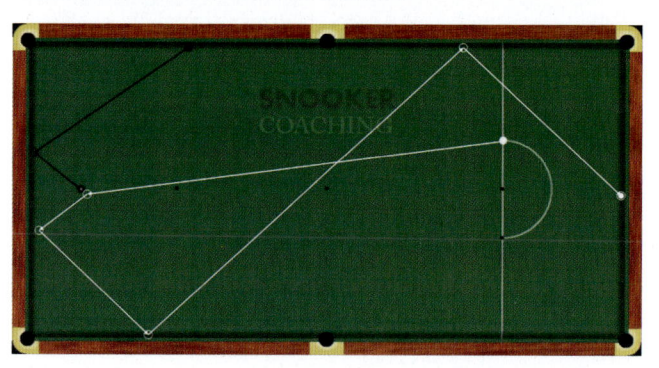

Fourth Shot – a tough one – thin edge of Red and back into baulk, covering the three Reds.

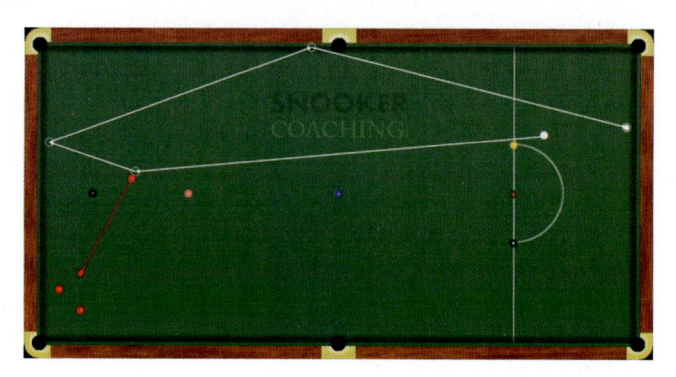

Fifth Shot – thin off Pink with White back to baulk and Pink behind Black.

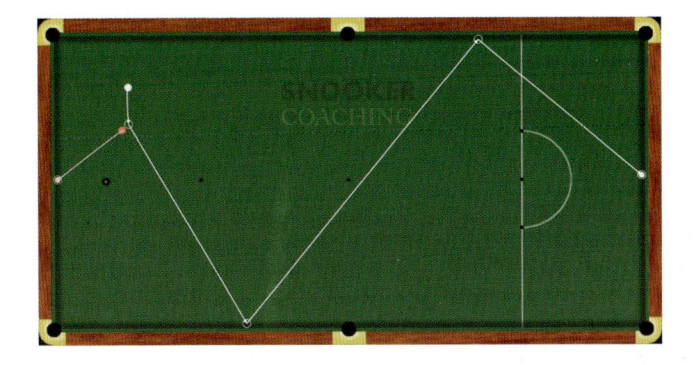

Sixth Shot – tough one – double Red into pack and White back to baulk behind Green.

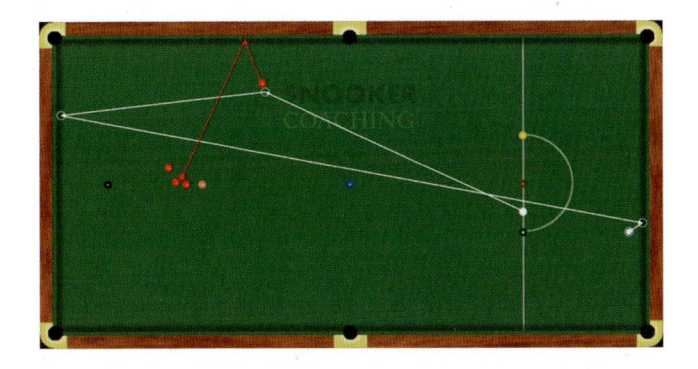

Seventh Shot – send Red up the table and White tucked in behind Pink and Yellow.

123

Eighth Shot – send the Black back to bottom cushion – almost a half-ball shot.

Ninth Shot – send White and Black to the side cushions.

Tenth Shot – send White thin off Black and tucked in behind Yellow and Brown.

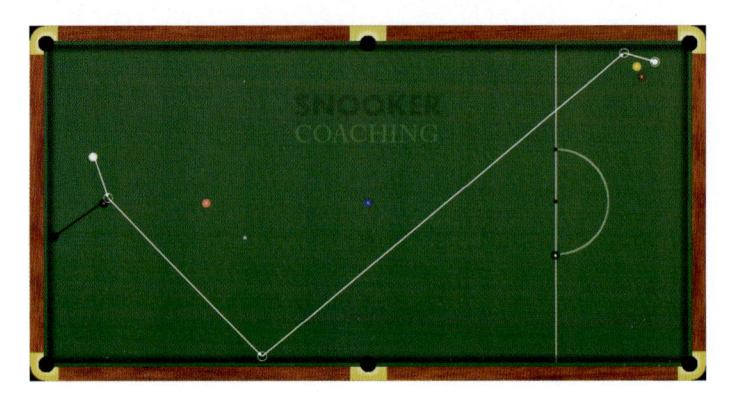

Safety off Black

Set balls as illustrated. Aim to send the Black ball to rest gently against the central Red on the bottom cushion. This is probably no longer the favoured safety shot of Black as it's been superseded by the following shot.

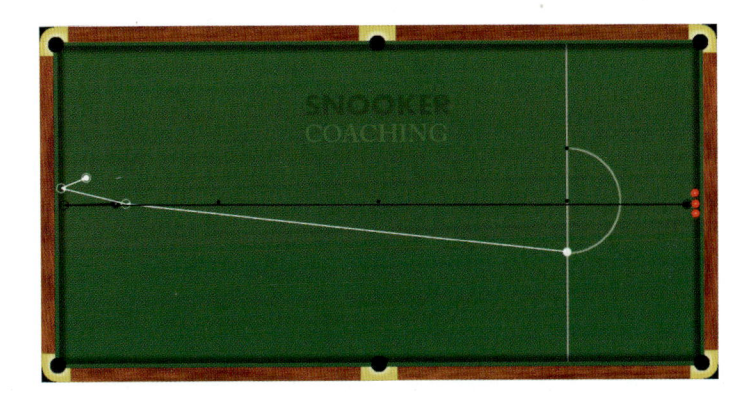

Safety off Black 2

Set balls as illustrated.
   Place the Cue ball on the Yellow spot and hit a slow drag shot, placing the white and Black to within an inch of each side cushion, as indicated by the Red balls.
   This is a half-ball shot and one that's favoured by the pros when it gets to a re-spotted Black.

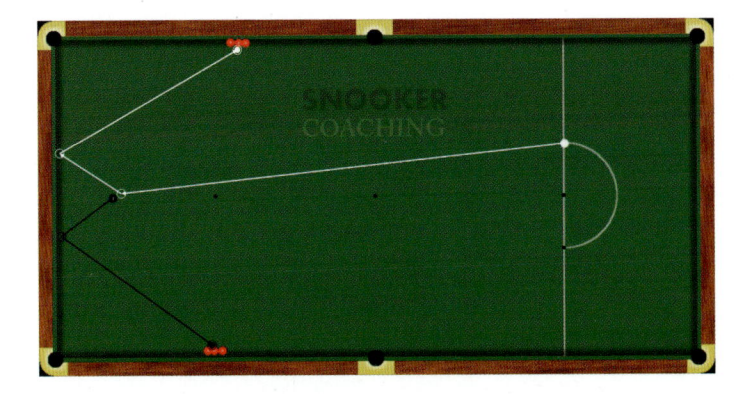

Reply to Safe Black

Set balls as illustrated.
 This is pretty much the standard reply that you will see the professional players use. Aim to send Black to the position indicated, and white to the position indicated. A useful reply to the above safety. Not the only one but often the one chosen by the better players, as with practice it is reliable under pressure.

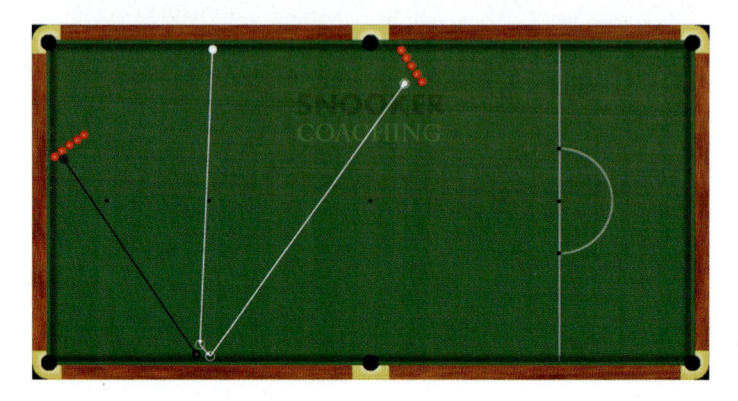

Key Shots on Brown

All the following shots are well known to the proficient player, and are part of the reason they clear the colours with such consistency.
 Set the balls as illustrated.
 When just off straight no side is required, it's just a plain ball off one cushion for position on Brown. This one you have practised many times in previous exercises, so don't miss.

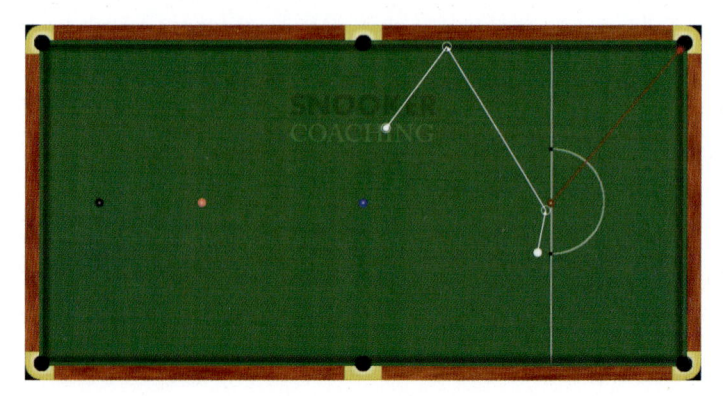

Set the balls as illustrated.
When slightly further out you will need just a trace of running side to gain position on Blue. This one you have practised many times in previous exercises, so don't miss.

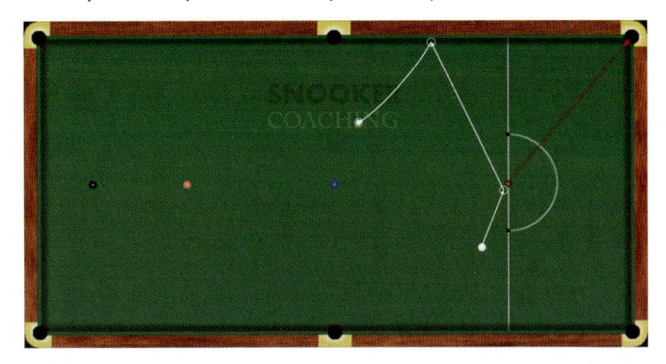

Set the balls as illustrated.
When slightly further out you will need to play a stun shot coming off the cushion for position on Blue. This one you have practised many times in previous exercises, so don't miss.

Set the balls as illustrated.
When further out and almost straight you can screw to the other side of Blue. This one you have practised many times in previous exercises, so don't miss.

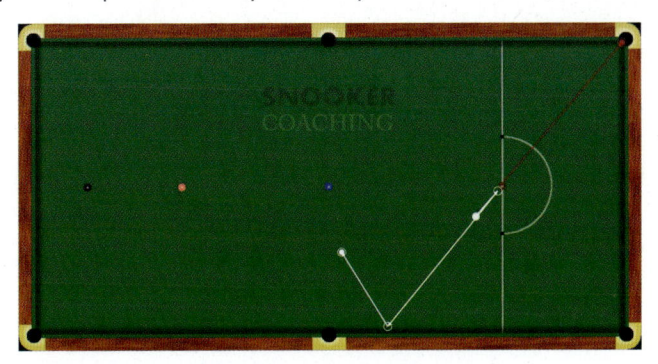

High on Blue

Set the balls as illustrated.

This situation is when you end up on the wrong side of Blue, which we have all done. The first situation is when you have a 3/4 ball pot. Play very high on the Cue ball with no side required to come off three cushions for position on Pink. Also from the same position, you can strike the Cue ball in the centre to come off the bottom cushion for position on Pink.

There are other more complicated possibilities, but this is the simplest and most used method to gain position.

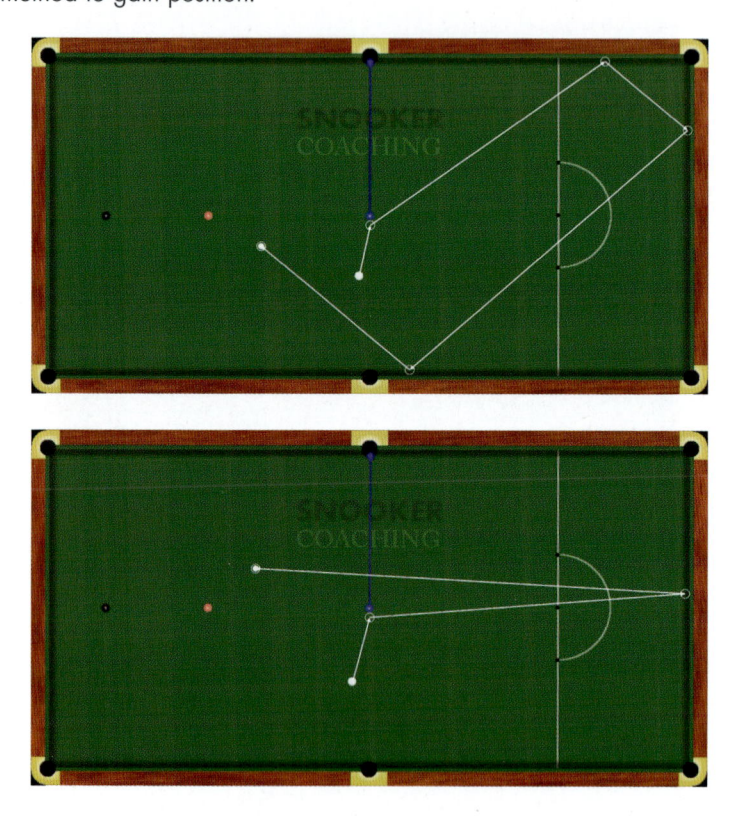

High on Blue

Set the balls as illustrated.
   This situation is when you end up on the wrong side of Blue.
   This situation is when you have about a 1/2 ball pot. Play high on the Cue ball, striking around the 11 o'clock position and cue smoothly rather than hitting hard, coming off two cushions for position on Pink. Also from this 1/2 ball situation, you can play a stun shot hitting just below the centre of the Cue ball to come off the bottom cushion for position on Pink.
   There are other more complicated possibilities, but this is the simplest and most used method to gain position.

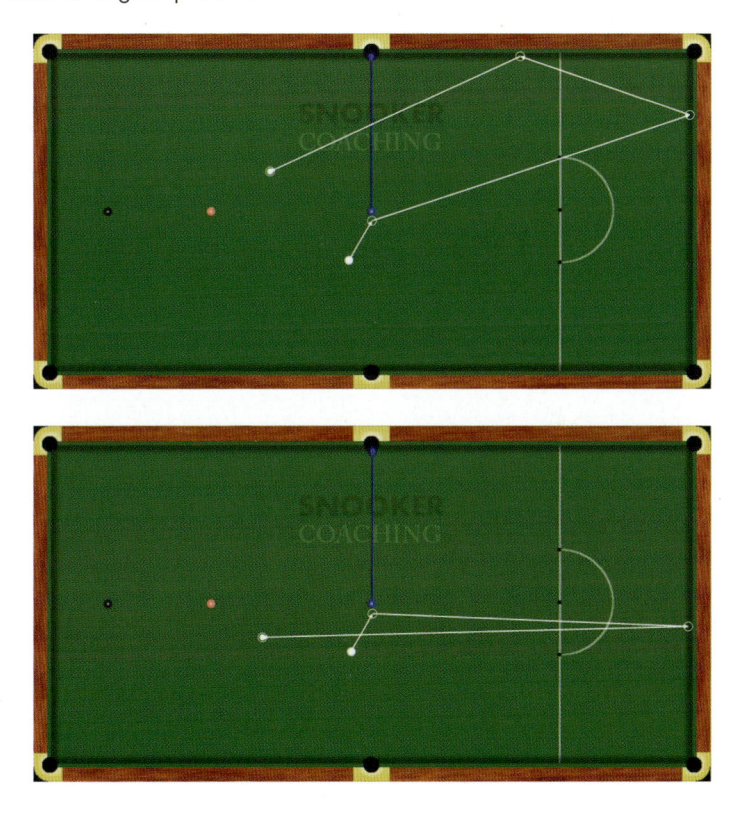

High on Blue

Set the balls as illustrated.

This situation is when you end up on the wrong side of Blue.

This situation is when you have about a 1/4 ball pot. This is a similar position to the half ball pot, but this time, as it is thinner, just hit a little lower than on the previous shot for position on Pink. Also from this situation, you can play a screw shot with no side to come off the bottom cushion for position on Pink.

There are other more complicated possibilities, but this is the simplest and most used method to gain position.

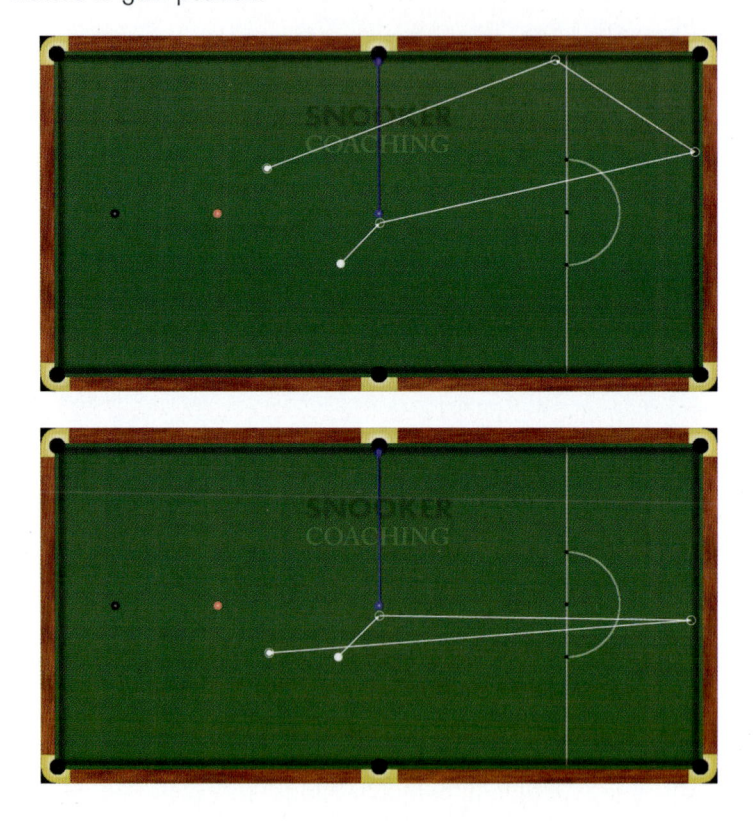

Then finish this practice on the Blue ball by completing three of each of the separate pots you have practised in the lesson.

Shots on the Pink

Set the balls as illustrated.
　From this position, you are slightly underside of the Pink, so you will need to play off two cushions to gain position for Black – no side, just top.

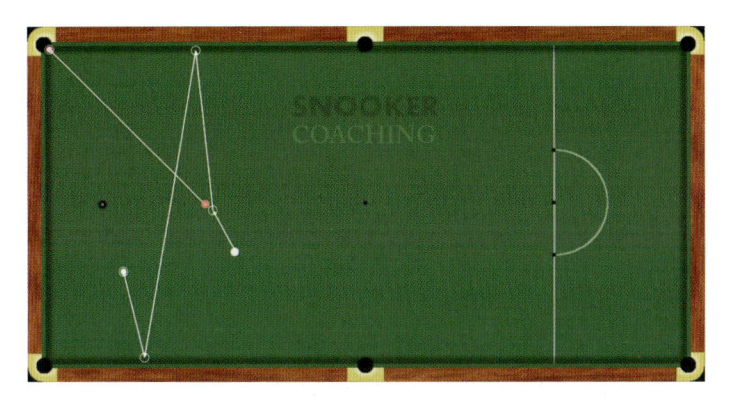

Shots on the Pink

Set the balls as illustrated.
　From this position, you are very low on the Pink, so you will need to play off four cushions and strike the Cue ball at 1 o'clock to gain position for Black.
　Not as easy as it seems and one to practise.

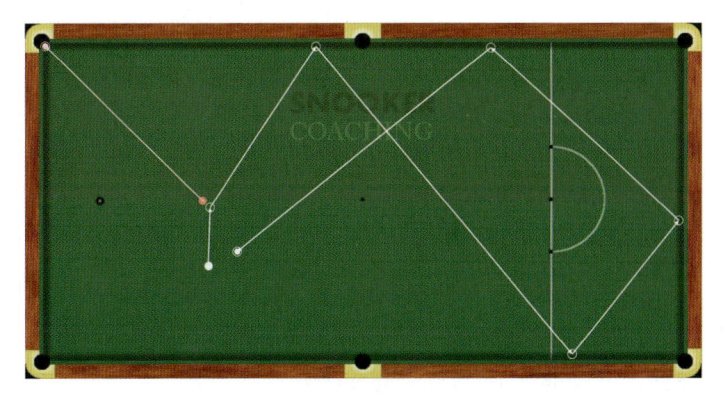

Pot Black and Screw

Set the balls as illustrated.
   You have practised this shot earlier on in the book, so test yourself!
   Pot the Black and screw for position on the Red on the Pink spot. Pot the Red. If you can, off the pot on the Red Ball try to gain position on Black.

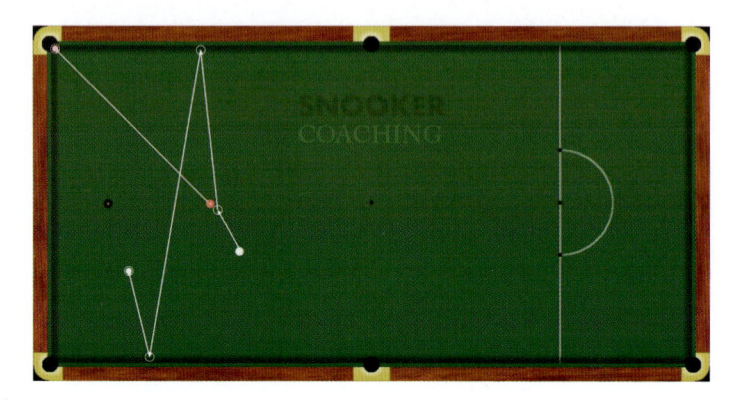

Pot Pink and Black

Set the balls as illustrated.
   Pot the Pink ball coming off two cushions for position on the Black ball. Pot the Black ball to complete the set.

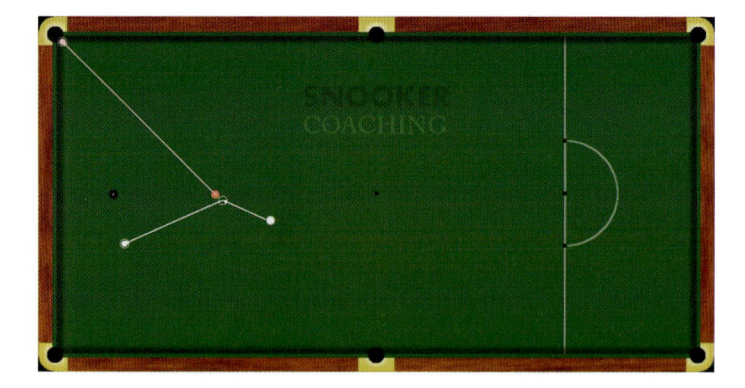

Pot and Follow

Set the balls as illustrated.
   You have practised this shot earlier on in the book, so test yourself!
   Pot the Pink and run through for position on the Black. Pot the Black.

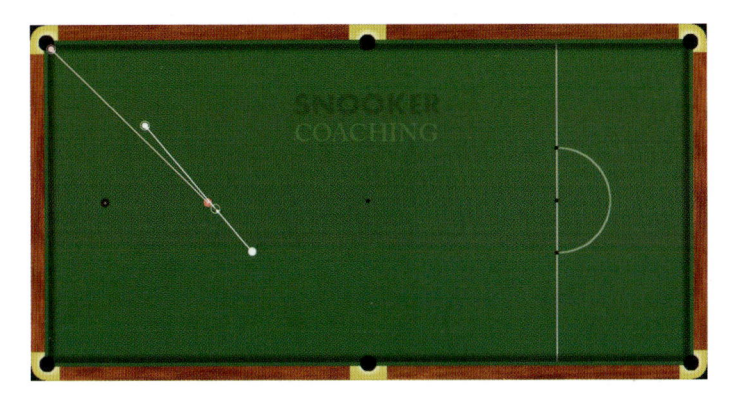

Stun Run

Set the balls as illustrated.
   You have practised this shot earlier on in the book, so test yourself!
   Pot the Blue and using stun run-through gain position to pot Black. Pot the Black.

Screw to Black

Set the balls as illustrated.
   You have practised this shot earlier on in the book, so test yourself!
   Pot the Red off the Blue spot and screw for position on the Black. Pot Black.

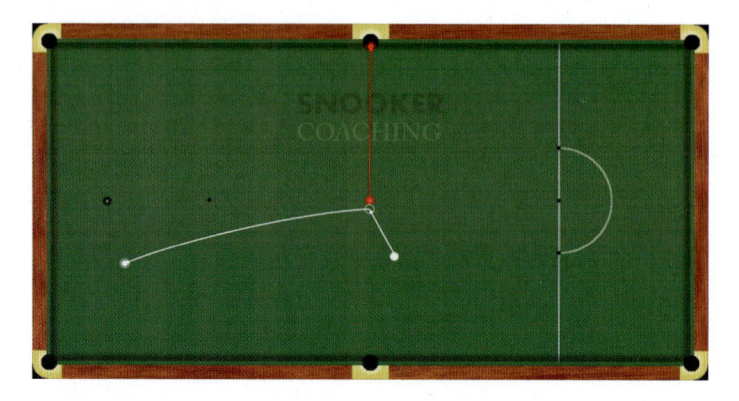

Easy Safety

Set the balls as illustrated.
   You have practised this shot earlier on in the book, so test yourself!
   From behind the Brown, aim to drop in dead-weight into the back of the pack.

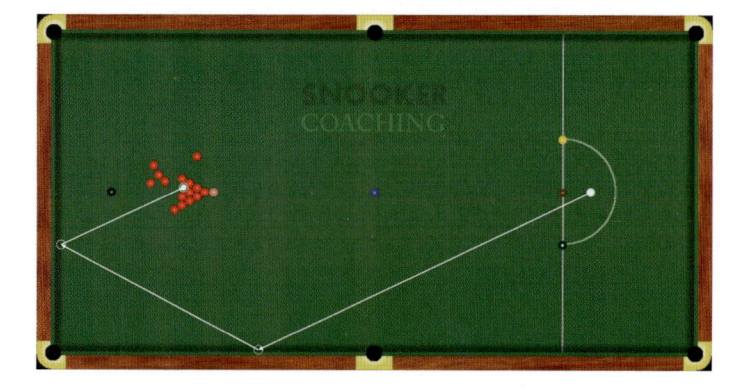

The Cross Double Safety

Set balls as illustrated.
You have practised this shot earlier on in the book, so test yourself!
Hitting just above the middle of the Cue ball aim to send the Black off the side cushion and onto the top cushion with the Cue ball into baulk.

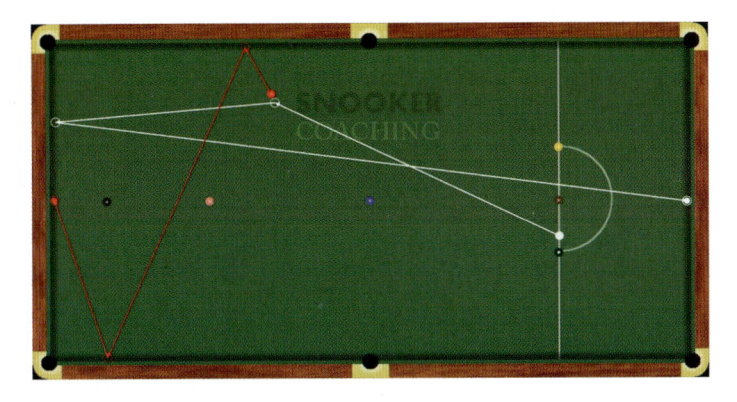

Position on Black from Green

Set the balls as illustrated.
You have practised this shot earlier on in the book, so test yourself!
Aim to pot Red, coming off two side cushions for position to pot Black.

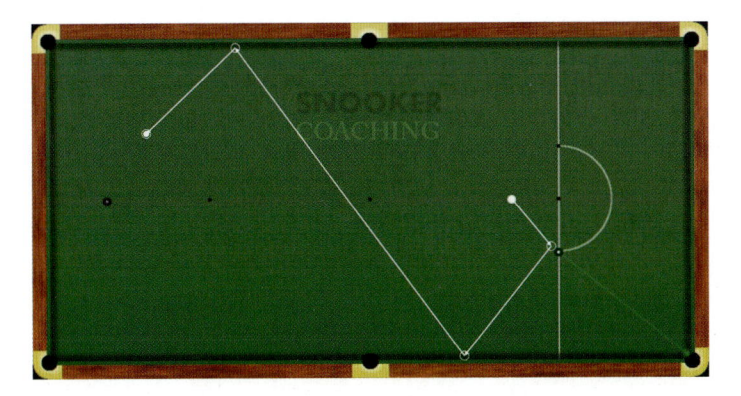

Black to Yellow

Set balls as illustrated.
   You have practised this shot earlier on in the book, so test yourself!
   Pot Black, stunning off the top and side cushions for position on Yellow. Pot Yellow.

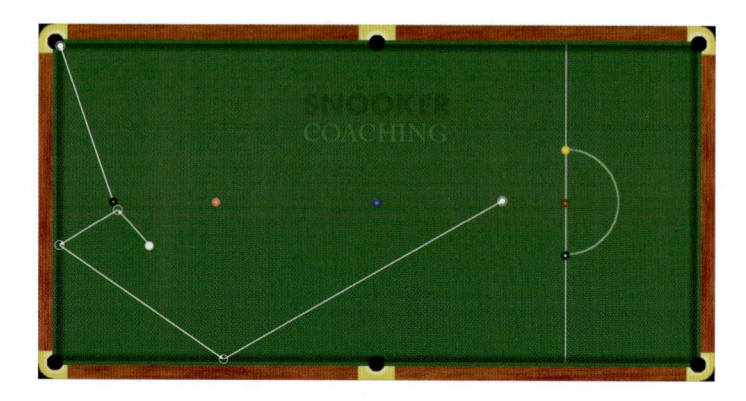

Black to Yellow

Set balls as illustrated.
   You have practised this shot earlier on in the book, so test yourself!
   Pot Black, running off the top and side cushions for position on Yellow. Pot Yellow.

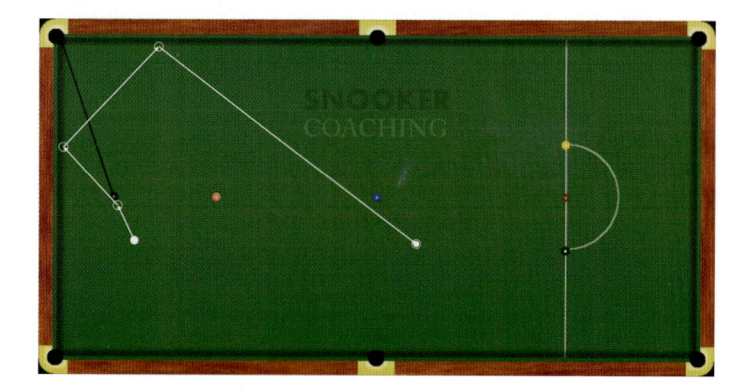

Pink to Yellow

Set balls as illustrated.

You have practised this shot earlier on in the book, so test yourself!

Pot Pink, running off the top and side cushions for position on Yellow. Pot Yellow.

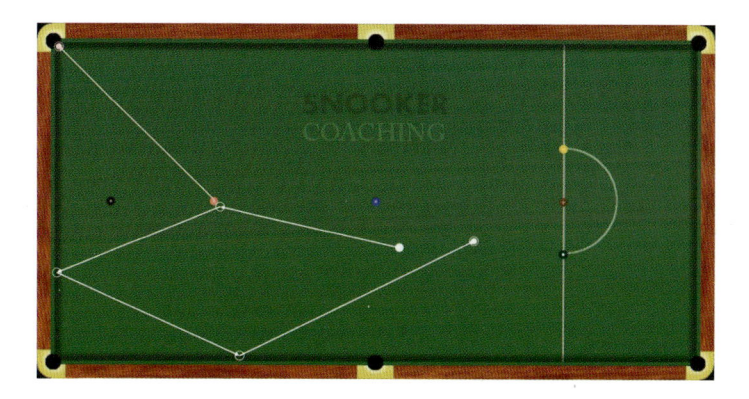

Pot and Cannon

Set the balls as illustrated.

You have practised this shot earlier on in the book, so test yourself!

Pot Blue and cannon into Red on the side cushion.

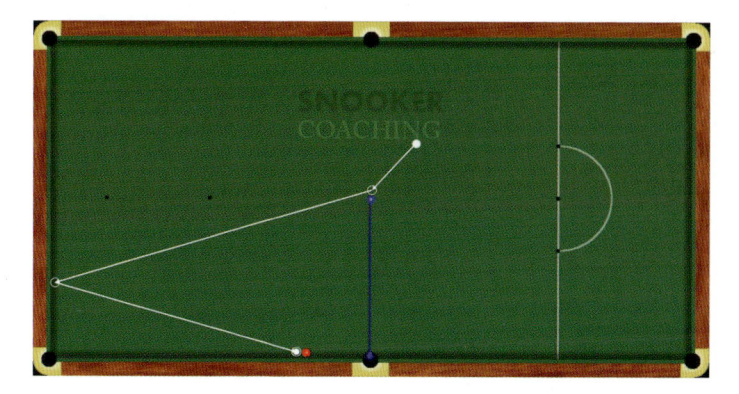

Brown to Black

Set the balls as illustrated.
   You have practised this shot earlier on in the book, so test yourself!
Pot Brown, gaining position to pot Black. Pot Black.

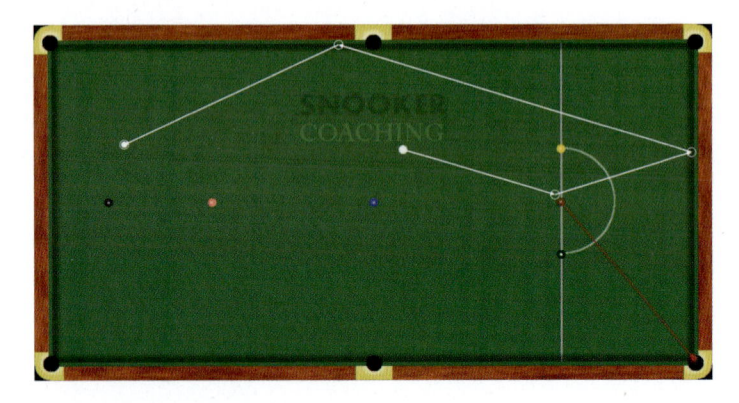

Wrong Side of Blue

Set the balls as illustrated.
   Using left-hand running side almost a screw shot to go between Brown and Yellow then off two cushions to come up the table.

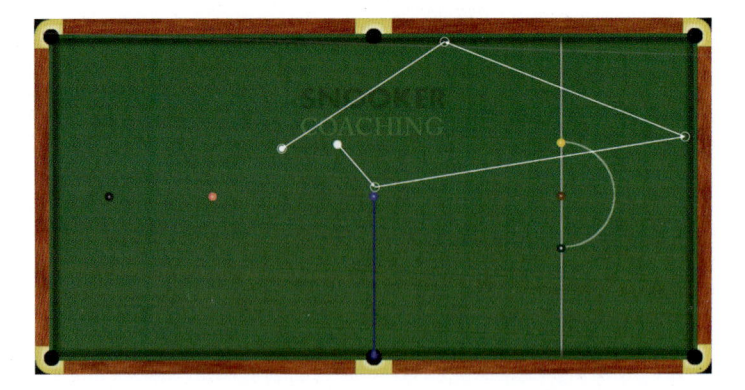

Wrong Side of Blue

Set the balls as illustrated.

Striking low but not hard and with right-hand running side come between Brown and Green then off two cushions to come up the table.

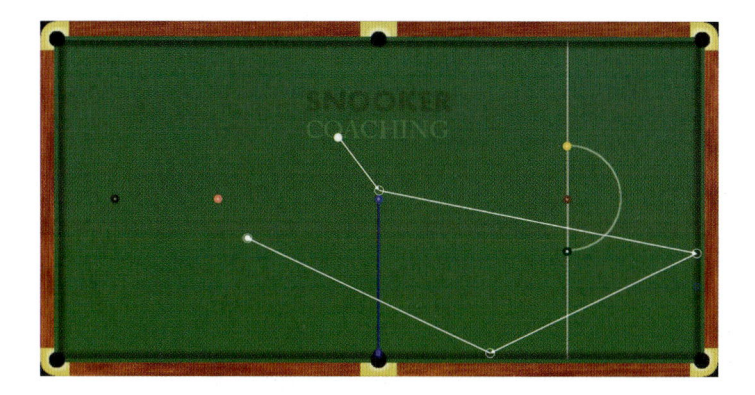

You can also play this shot by striking plain ball just below centre to come off the bottom cushion between Brown and Green then up the table, just missing Green.

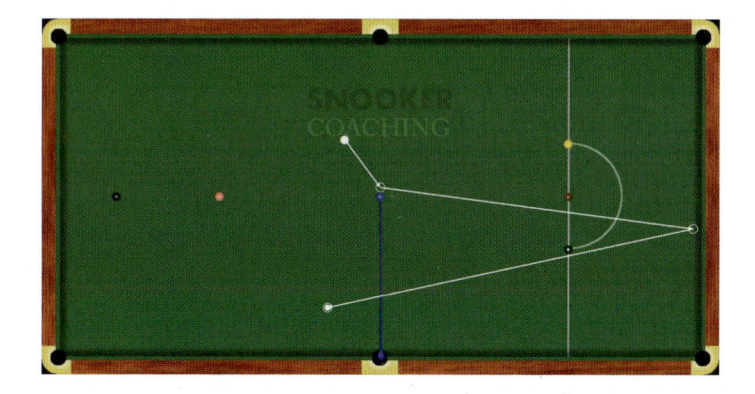

Again, this shot can be played in a different way by using check side to go between and come back between Brown and Green.

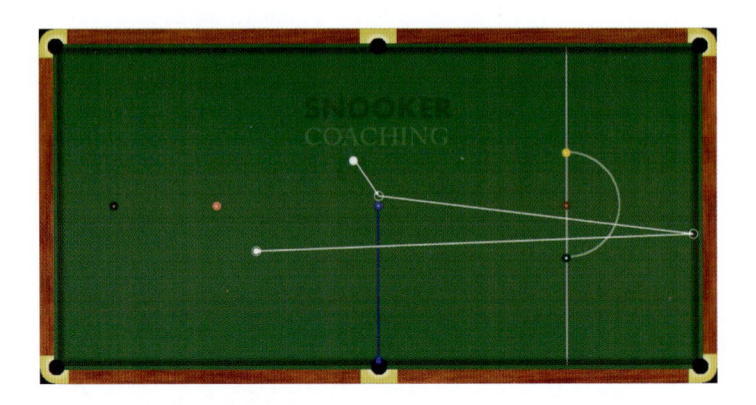

Brown to Blue Shots

The following sequence of shots is ones that all proficient players know how to play. There are other ways of playing the shots, but these are recognized as the easiest.

Set the balls as illustrated.

Play a straight screw shot to gain position on Blue – practise from both sides of the table.

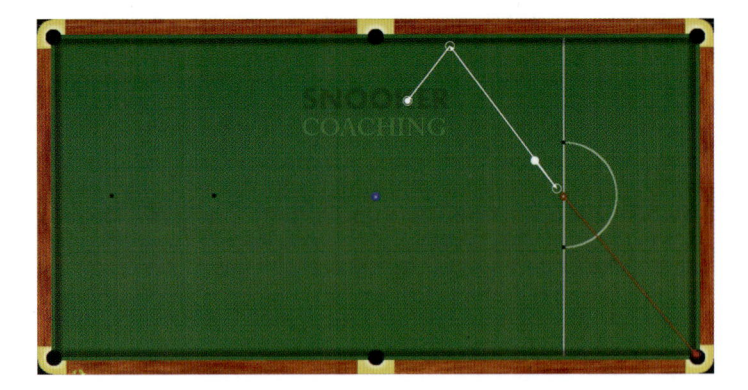

Brown to Blue Shots

Set the balls as illustrated.

This is about a 3/4 ball shot and is a forcing stun shot to move the White into position for Blue without using a cushion.

All proficient players can play this shot, but it's one that requires considerable practice to be consistent.

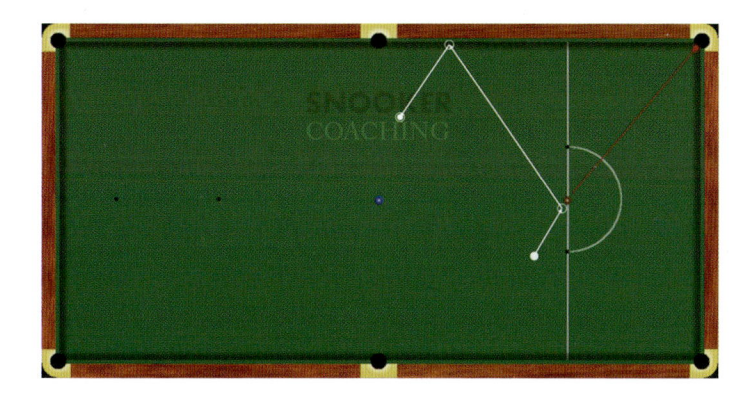

This shot can also be played as a screw shot to come back into position for Blue – no need to play hard, just a nice follow-through with smooth cueing.

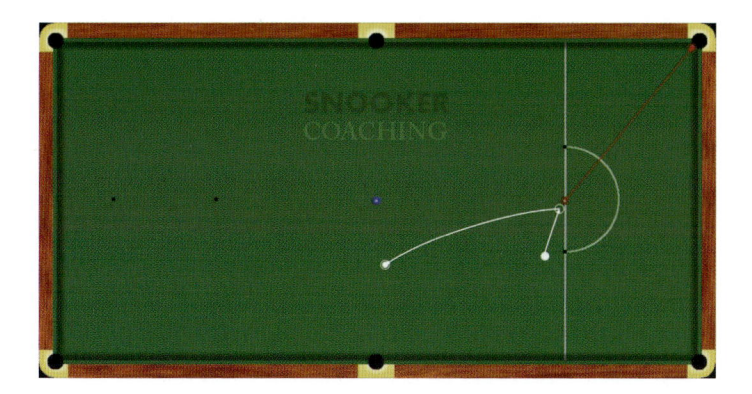

Brown to Blue Shots

Set the balls as illustrated.
   This is about a 1/2 ball stun shot using the side cushion to gain position for Blue.
   This shot is a basic that all proficient players have spent many hours in trying to master.

Brown to Blue Shots

Set the balls as illustrated.
   This is about a 1/4 ball shot and is gentle screw shot, not using any cushion, and gaining position for Blue.
   This is a tough shot, and over the years even my best students have not found this easy.

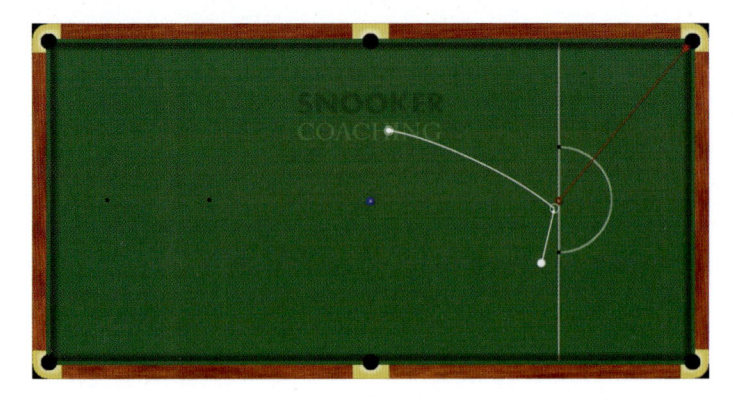

Brown to Blue Shots

Set the balls as illustrated.
   This is about a 3/4 ball shot and is a run-through shot striking the Cue ball at 11 o'clock to move the White into position for Blue.

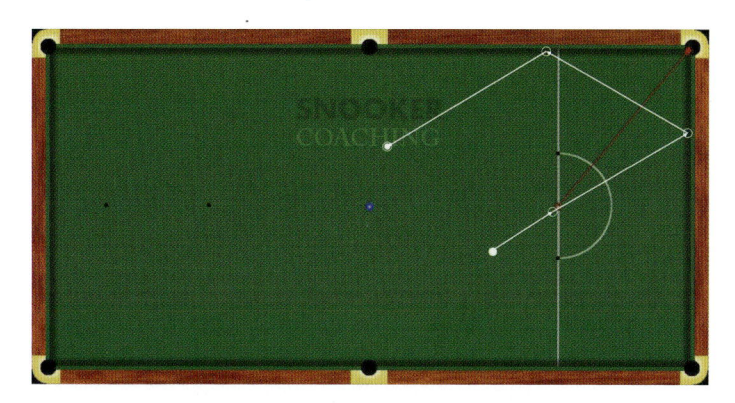

Brown to Blue Shots

Set the balls as illustrated.
   This is about a 1/2 ball where you will need to use the rest to stun off the bottom and side cushion to gain position for Blue.

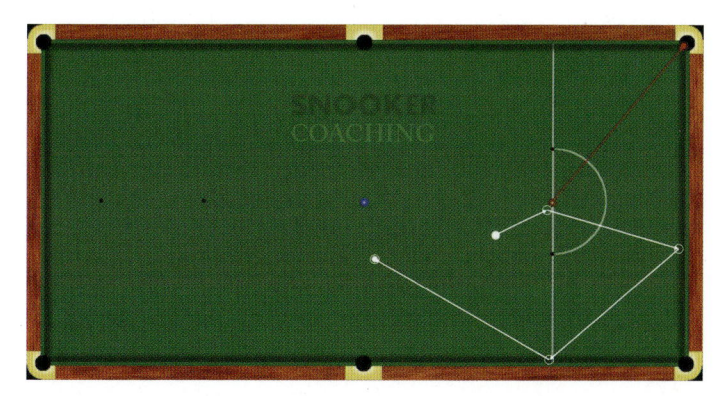

Brown to Blue Shots

Set the balls as illustrated.

This is about a 1/4 ball shot where no side is required to come off the bottom and side cushion to gain position for Blue.

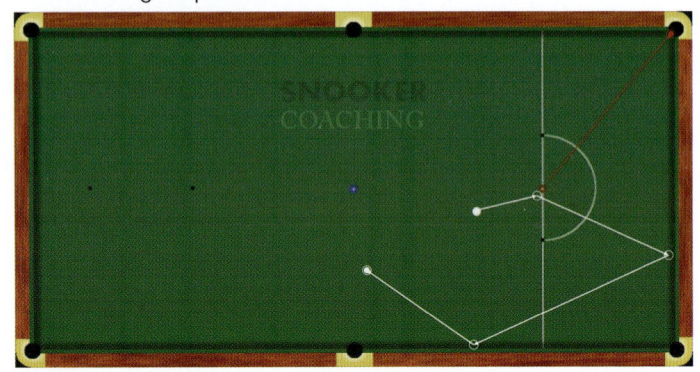

The Complete Shots

Starting with the first shot in the lesson, pot Brown and gain position on Blue, but this time, also pot Blue.

Do the same with each of the other shots off Brown, not moving on to the next shot until you have potted both Brown and Blue.

A Safety Shot

Set the balls as illustrated.

This is not an easy safety and needs considerable practice to become proficient, but a good one to have.

Aim to place the Red safe and White behind Black.

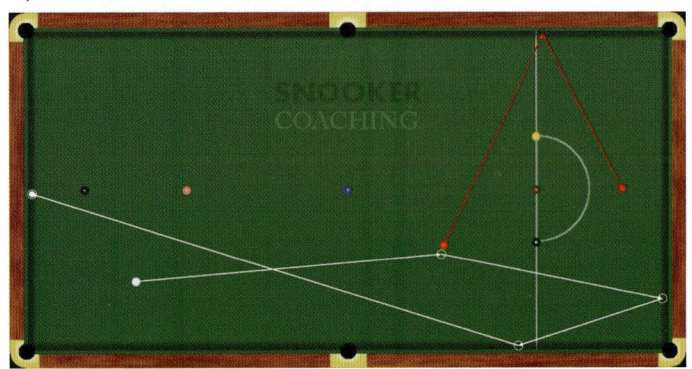

A Safety Shot

Set the balls as illustrated.
   This again is not an easy safety but once mastered you will always have it.
   Aim to place the Red safe and White behind Black.

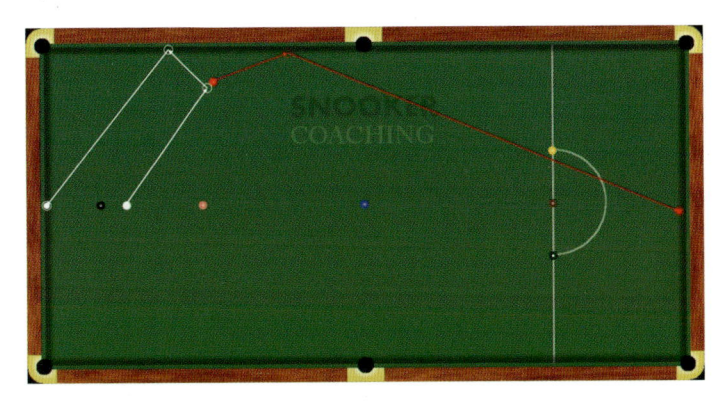

A Safety Shot

Set the balls as illustrated.
   This is not an easy safety and needs considerable practice to become proficient, but a good one to have.
   Aim to place the Red safe and white behind Black – you will notice that this time, the Red is close to the bottom cushion.

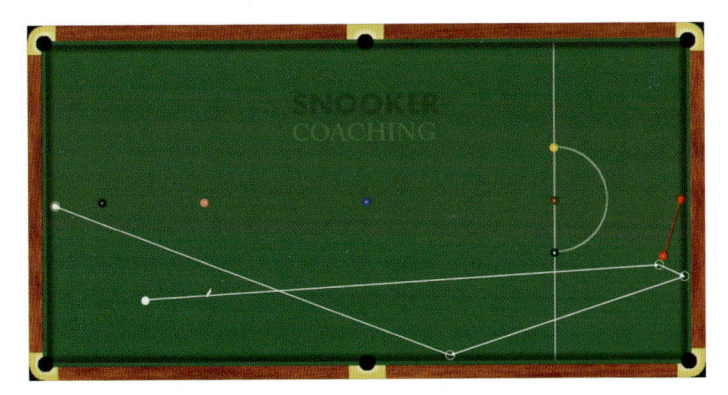

145

Almost Straight

This shot is often missed as players tend to think it's a bigger angle than it is.
Concentrate on hitting the object ball fuller.
Complete three pots in succession – miss and start again.

Safety – Red to Baulk

Set the balls as illustrated.
Aim to send the Red ball near to the bottom cushion as illustrated and the White ball to the top end of the table – tough, so concentrate!

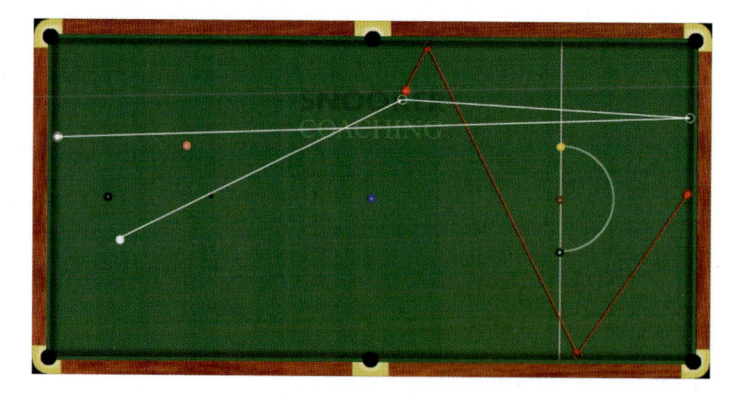

Safety Double

Set the balls as illustrated.
 Double the Red ball behind the Black ball and the White ball back into the baulk area.

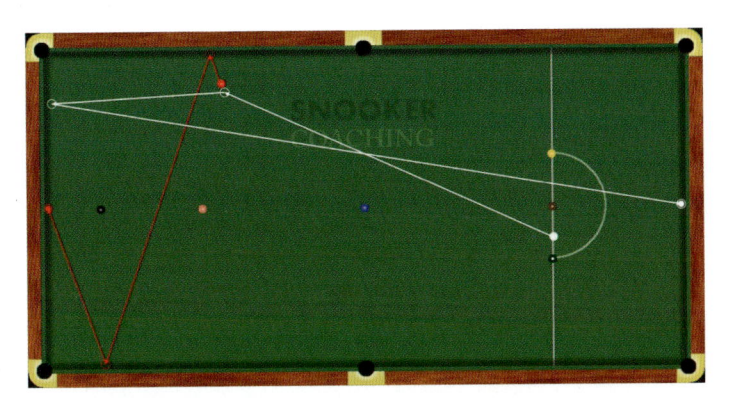

Safety – Loose Red

Set the balls as illustrated.
 Aim to drop onto the Red, hardly moving it at all.

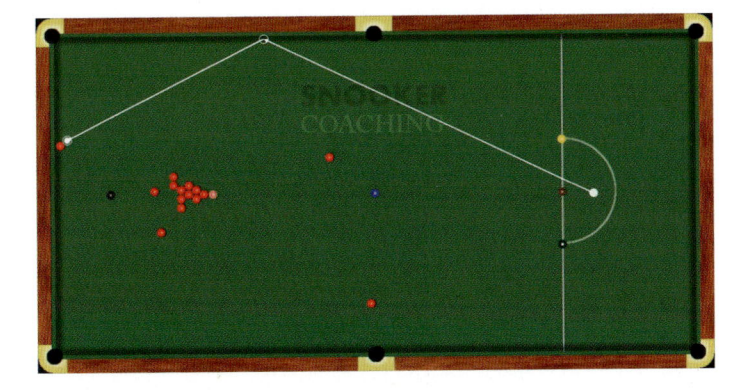

147

Safety – Red Behind Black

Set the balls as illustrated.
 Simple shot – send the Red ball behind the Black ball and the White ball into the baulk area as illustrated.

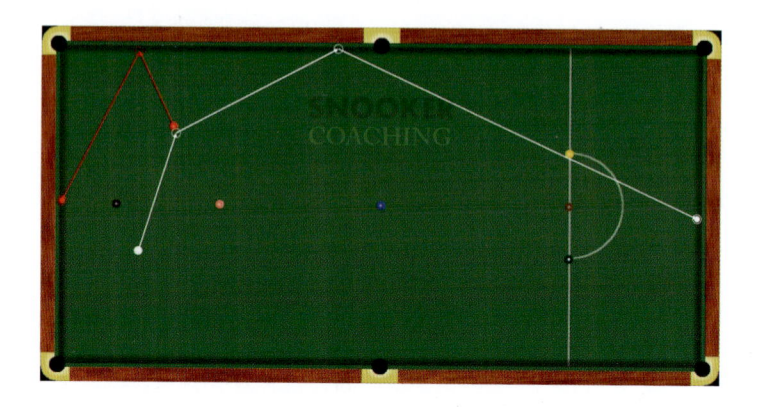

Safety – Cue Ball Behind Black

Set the balls as illustrated.
 Again quite a simple shot – simply send the Red ball into the baulk area and the White ball behind the Black ball.

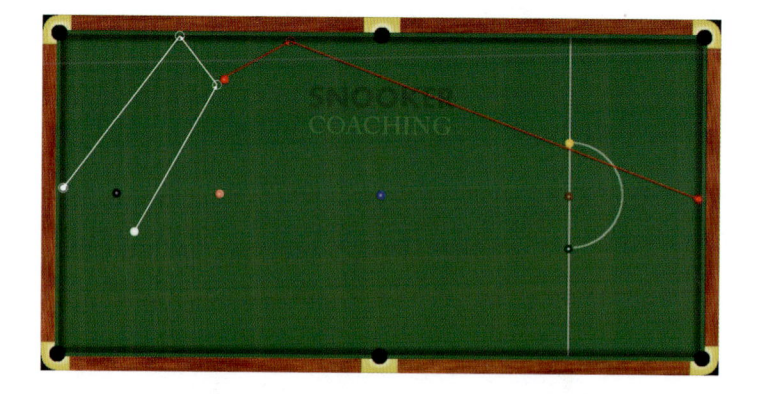

Safety – White Behind Black

Set the balls as illustrated.
    This is a tough shot and needs considerable practice to become proficient, but a good one to have. Aim to place the Red ball safe and the White ball behind the Black ball.

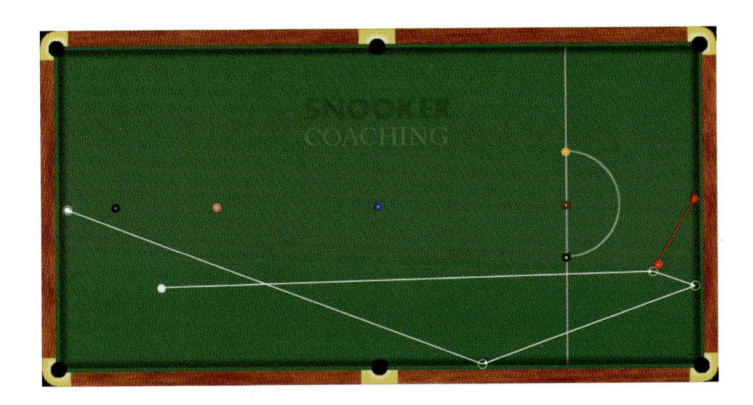

Power Run Through

Set the balls as indicated.
    Ensure you hit high on the Cue ball and smooth and powerful hitting through the ball.
    Try to get the Cue ball into the baulk area.

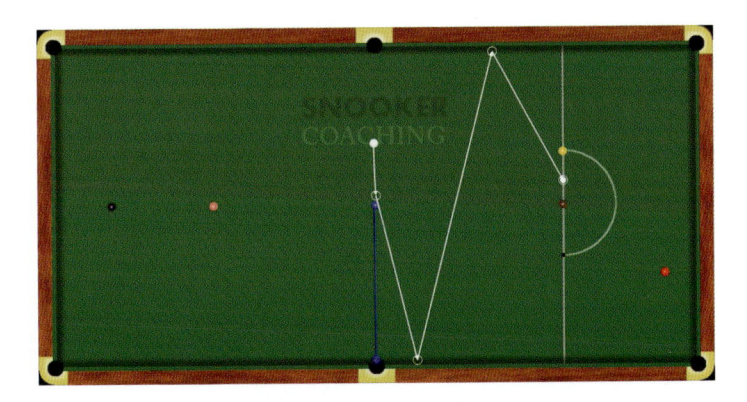

A variation of this is almost straight on Black. As above, to gain position for Yellow.

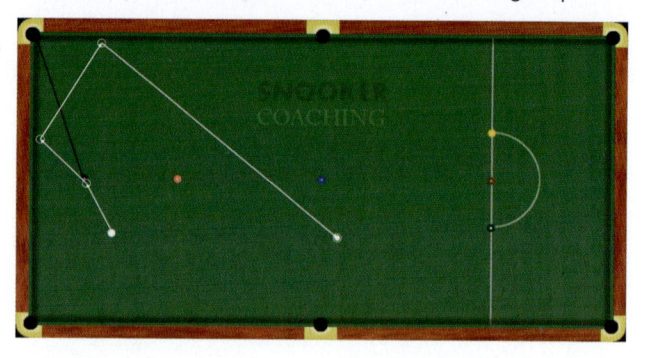

A Trace of Side

Set the balls as illustrated.
　Using just a trace of side, strike the Cue ball at 3 o'clock to gain a good position on the Red.

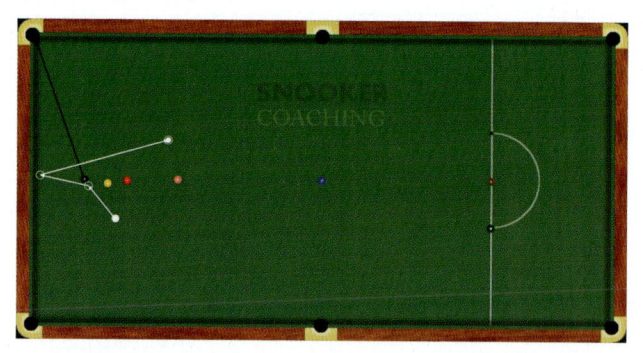

A Trace of Side 2

Set the balls as illustrated.
　Using just a trace of check, strike the Cue ball at 9 o'clock to gain good position on the Reds.

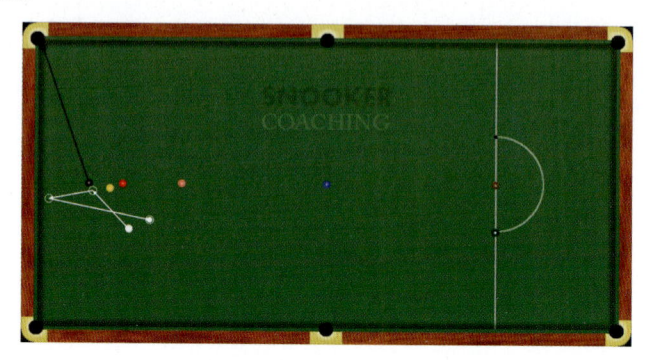

Aim to split the pack by hitting Pink full in the face.
On each occasion that you split the pack, continue and try to get a break above 50.

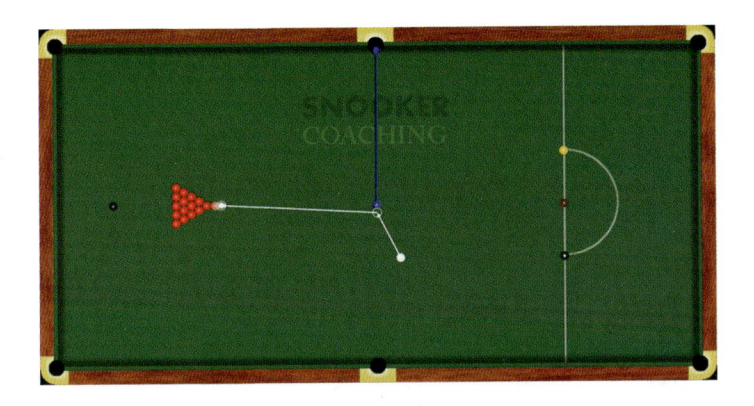

Angled Red

Set the balls as illustrated.
Pot the difficult Red, gaining position off the side cushion for Black. Pot Black.

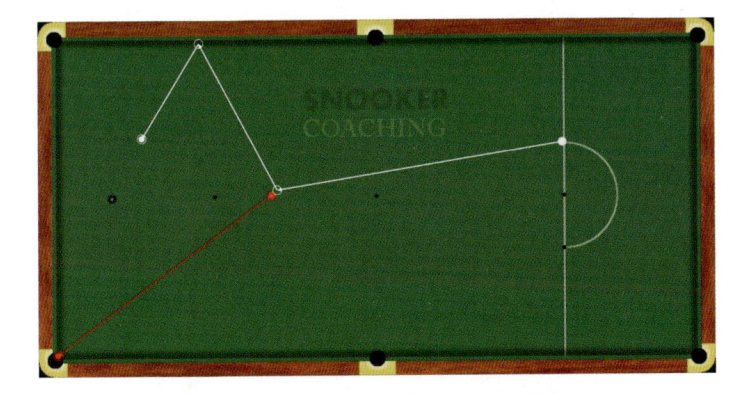

Potting to the Middle

Set the balls as illustrated.
   First shot when full ball, is a straight screw shot for position on Black. Pot Black.

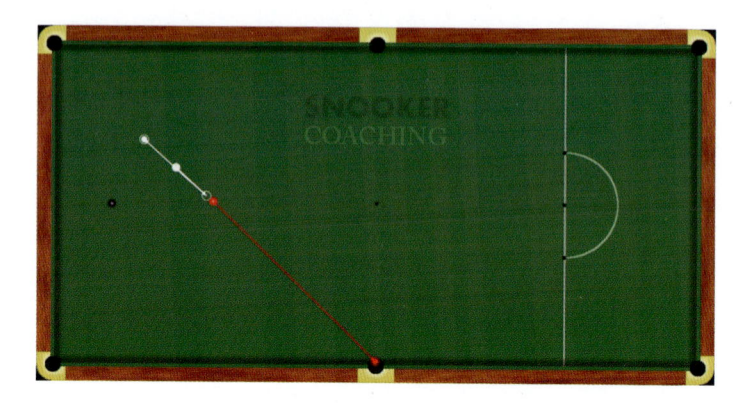

   Second shot is 3/4 ball shot, which you play as a stun shot for position on Black. Pot Black.
   Complete five times in succession – miss and start again.
   Spend 10 minutes on this exercise.

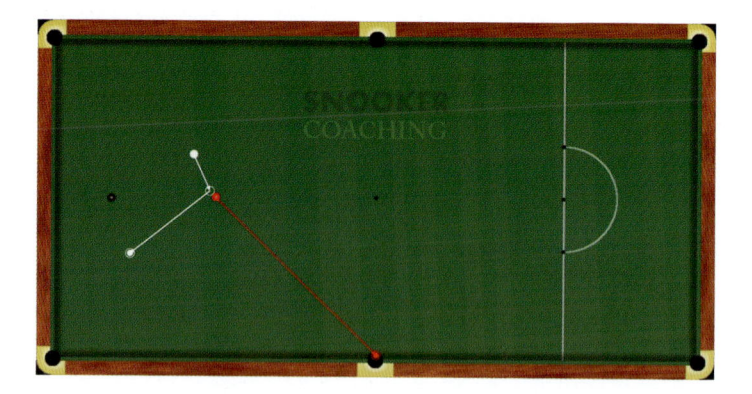

Third shot is a half ball and is a run-through shot for position on Black. Pot Black.
Complete five times in succession – miss and start again.
Spend 10 minutes on this exercise.

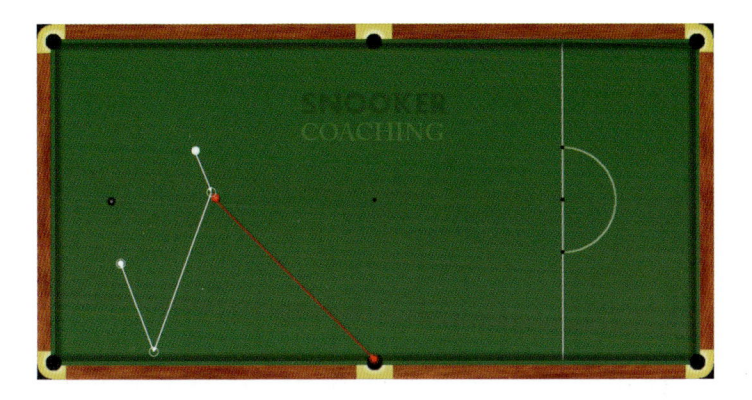

Fourth shot is 1/4 ball where you run around the other side of Black. Pot Black.
Complete five times in succession – miss and start again.
Spend 10 minutes on this exercise.

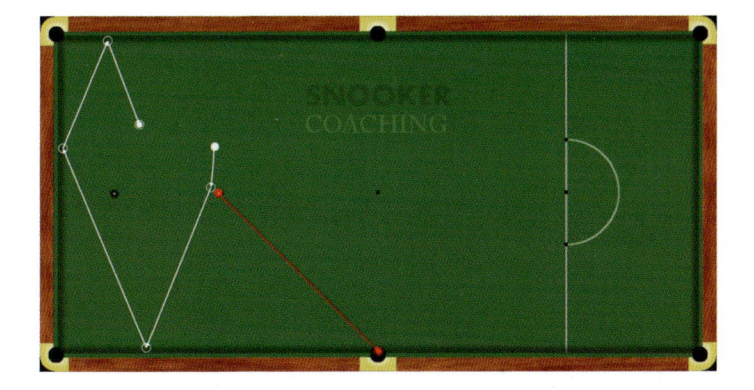

Escape Shot

Set the balls as illustrated. A well-known shot and easier than it looks when mastered.

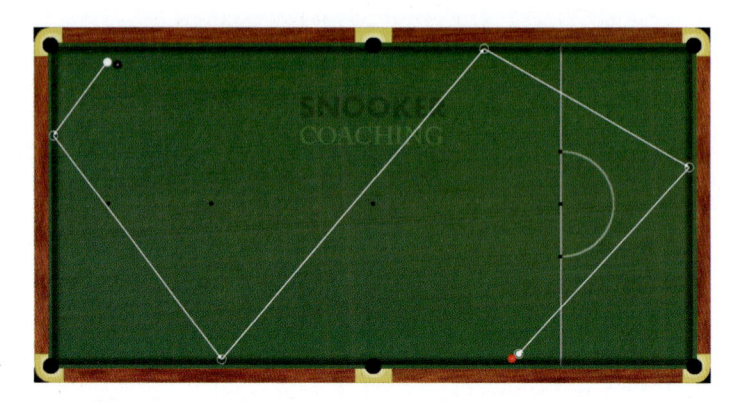

Escape Shot

Set the balls as illustrated. Another old-time favourite that sometimes is needed. Again, with this shot running side is required.

Escape Shot

Set the balls as illustrated. White just misses Blue to come off the side and top cushion for Red.
    A trace of running side is again needed for this shot.

Balls along the Cushion

Set the balls as illustrated.
    Playing this shot with no side, top spin, and pace to move into position for Black, which you pot.

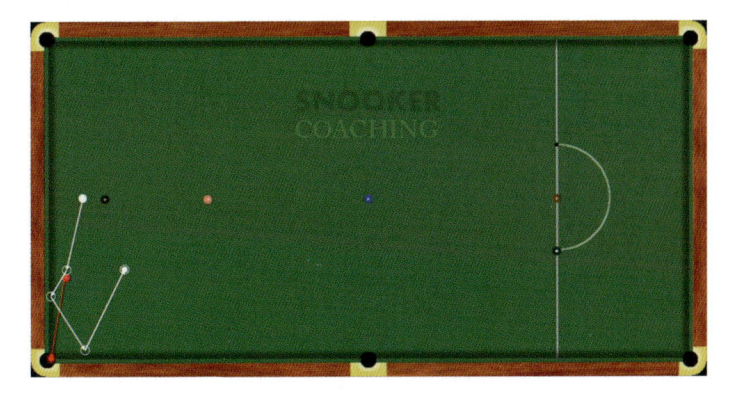

Balls along the Cushion

Set the balls as illustrated.
   Playing this shot is much easier as all you need to do is drop the ball in deadweight.

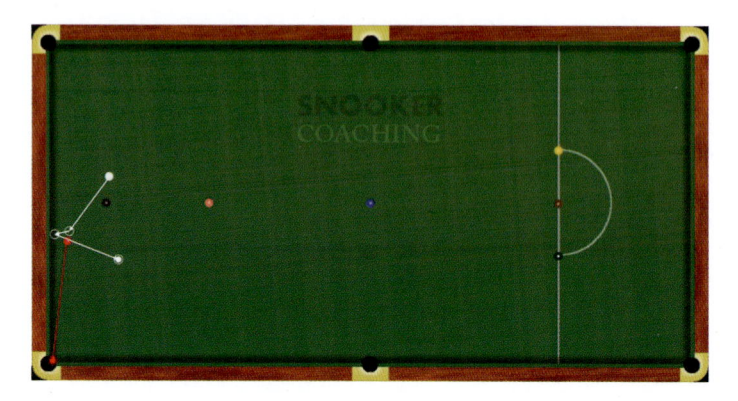

Balls along the Cushion

Set the balls as illustrated.
   Playing this shot is very tough and at best hit and miss, however, there is no other option than deep screw with reverse side.

Safety on Black

Set the balls as illustrated.
   Aim to send the Black off the top cushion and back within 1 inch of the baulk line.

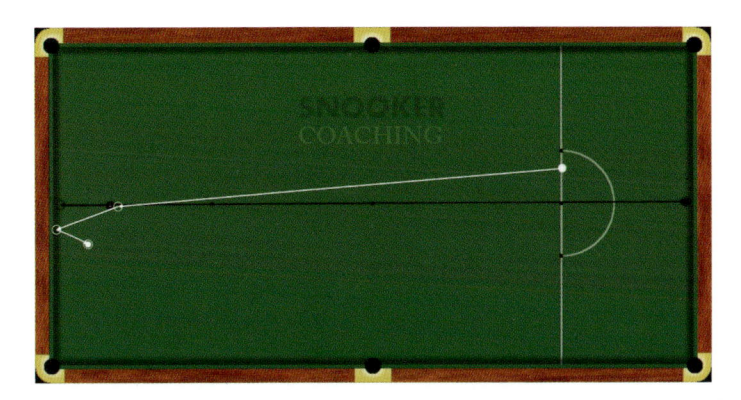

Splitting the Pack off Baulk Colours

Set the balls as illustrated.
   The purpose of this exercise is to split the pack of what is about a 1/4 ball pot on Yellow and to pot a Red.
   Hit at 7 o'clock, so just a trace of side.
   Complete the pot on Yellow, the split of the pack and pot on Red 10 times.

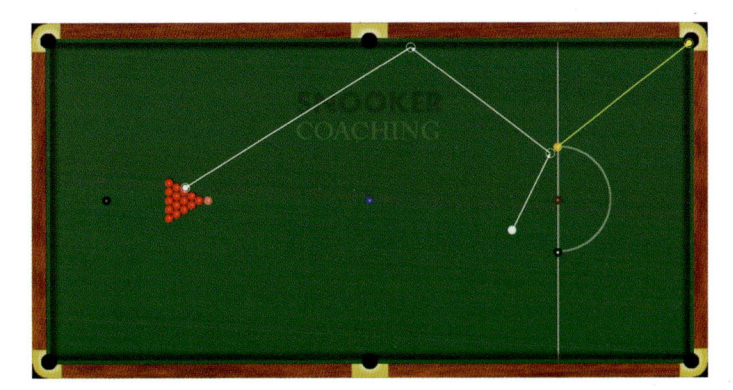

Splitting a Flat Pack

Set the balls as illustrated.

This is a powerful stun shot where you accelerate through the Cue ball and smash the middle of the pack.

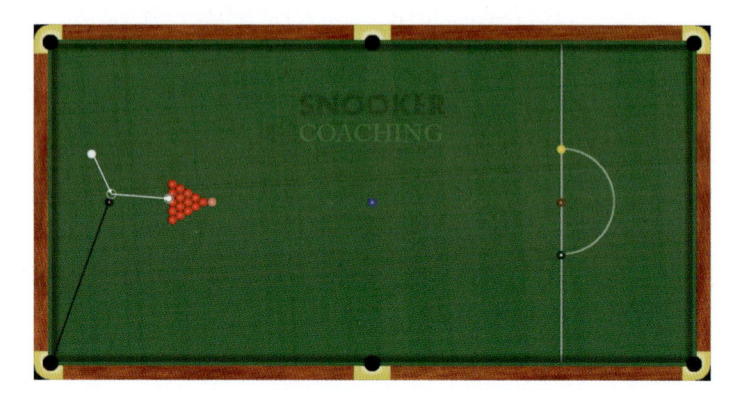

Splitting a Pack off the Back Cushion

Set the balls as illustrated.

This is a power run-through shot and about a half-ball pot on Black, striking high on the Cue ball to arc into the pack.

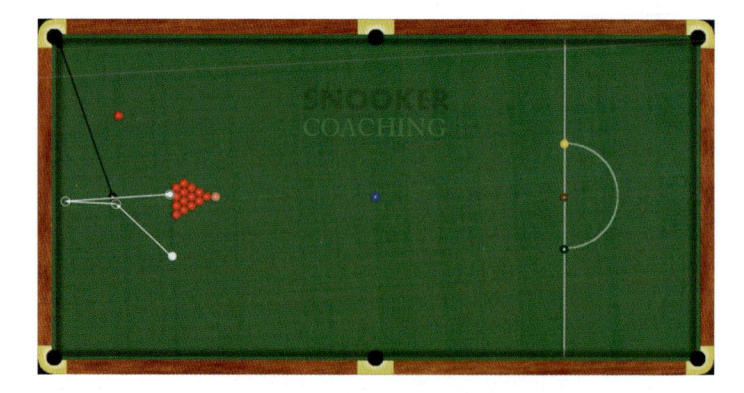

Blind-Pocket Pot

Set the balls as illustrated.
 Ensure you line up this shot in a semi-upright stance as you will not see the pocket when down.

Fun off the Pink

Set the balls as illustrated.
 Striking the ball at 1 o'clock, play off four cushions to gain position on Black. Pot Black.

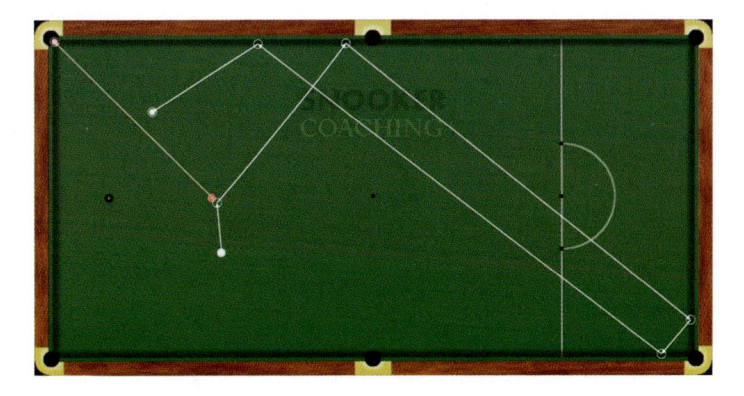

Soft Screw on Black

Set the balls as illustrated.
From this low position on Black, you can only play a soft screw shot or the spin does not have time to work.

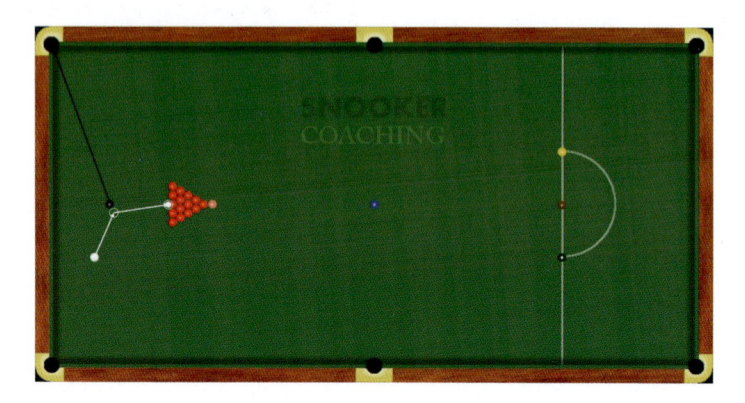

Pot and Run

From this position, it's safer to pot the Red to middle and send the White ball off the top cushion for position on the Black ball rather than just dropping it in.

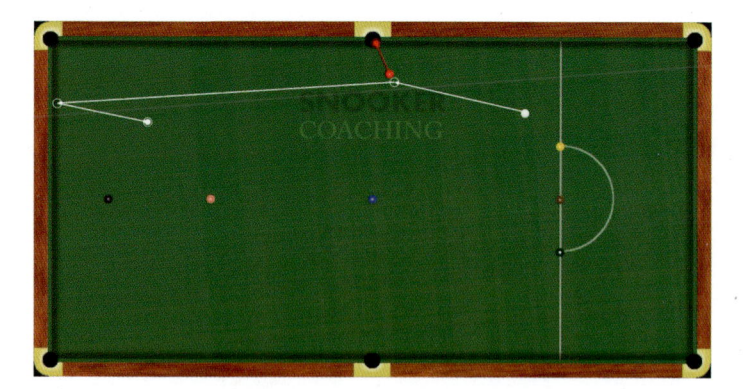

Black to Yellow

This is a sequence of shots that all proficient players are familiar with and use. There are numerous other ways to play the shots, but the following are recognized as the easiest and are the ones I have used and taught for many years.

Set the balls as illustrated.

Position 1 – This is dead straight, so screw back with reverse side. Pot Yellow.

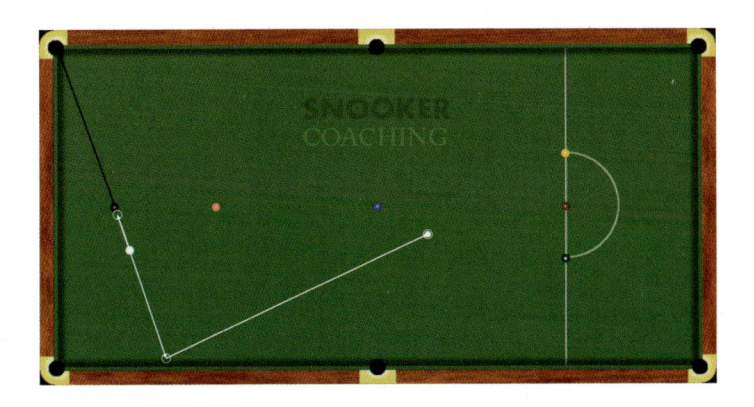

Position 2 – This is a 3/4 ball shot that needs to be struck at 1 o'clock to run through for Yellow.

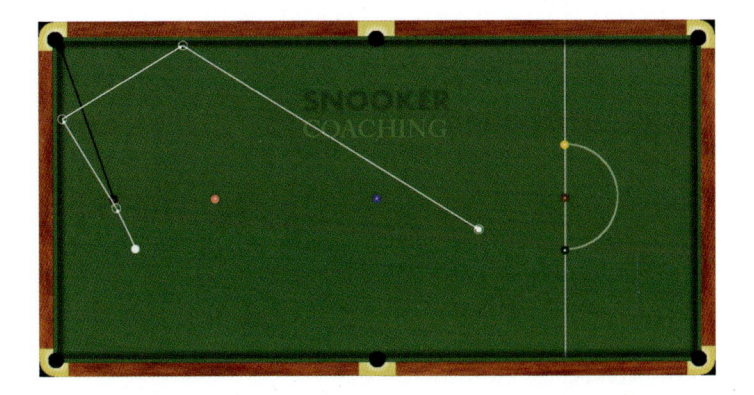

161

Position 3 – This is a 1/2 ball stun shot off the top and side cushion – no side needed.

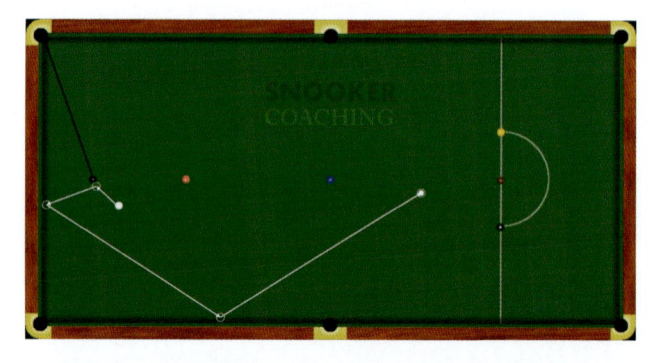

Position 4 – This is a 1/4 ball stun shot hitting low to stun off two cushions.

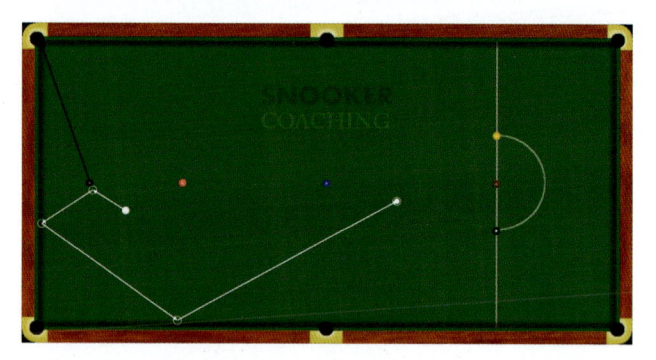

Shots from the Opposite Side

Set the balls as illustrated.

Position 1 – This is dead straight, so screw back with reverse side. Pot Yellow.

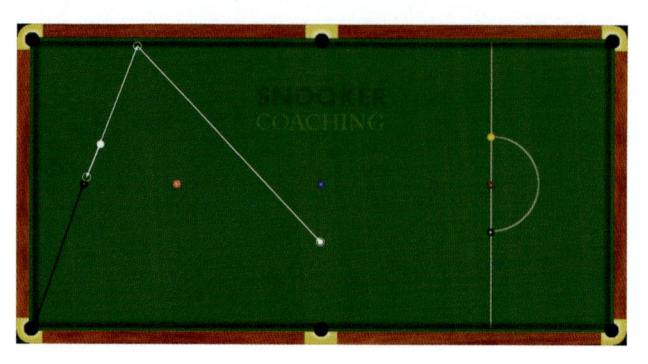

Position 2 – This is a 3/4 ball shot that needs top and running side to run through off the top and side cushions for Yellow.

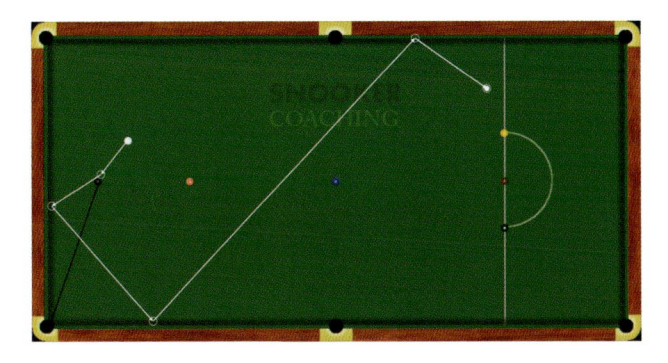

Position 3 – This is a simple 1/2 ball shot off the top cushion – no side needed.

Position 4 – This is a 1/4 ball shot which needs a trace of side, so strike at 11 o'clock to follow a similar line as the 1/2 ball shot.

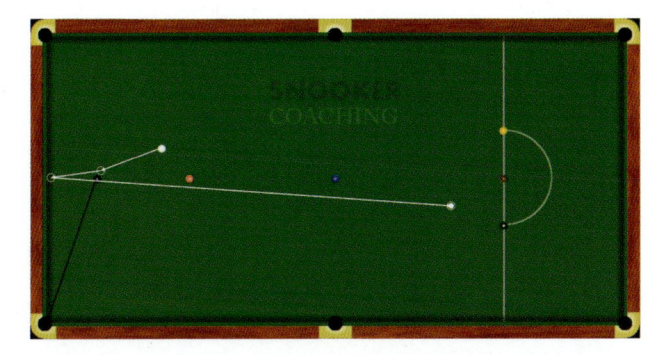

Black to Yellow Shots

Again, more shots that all proficient players know and use. There are numerous ways to play the following shots, but these are the easiest and are the ones I have used and taught for many years.

Set the balls as illustrated.

Position 1 – This is dead straight, so screw back with reverse side. Pot Yellow.

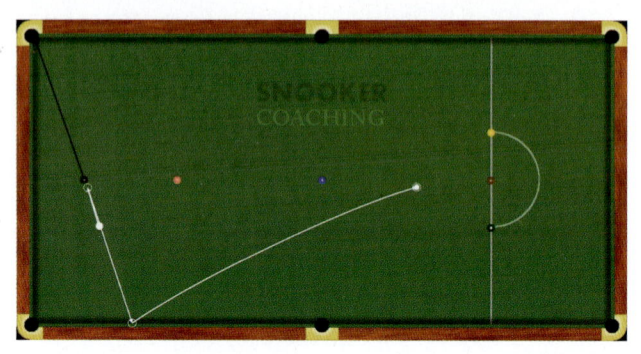

Position 2 – Slightly lower than position 1 becomes a run-through shot off the side cushion.

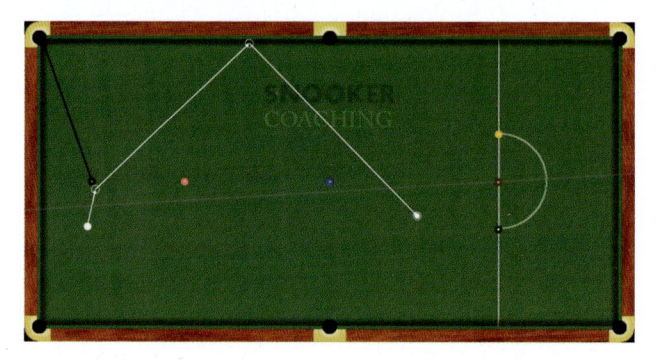

Position 3 – Lower still becomes a stun shot off the side cushion for Yellow into Green pocket.

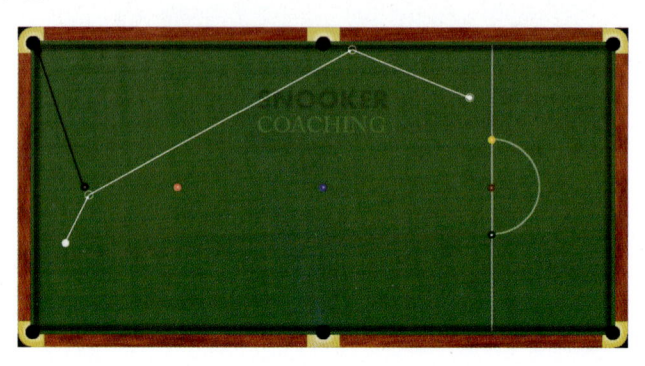

Position 4 – Even lower becomes screw with a trace of side, so strike at 5 o'clock to come off the side cushion and bottom cushion between Yellow and Green for position on Yellow.

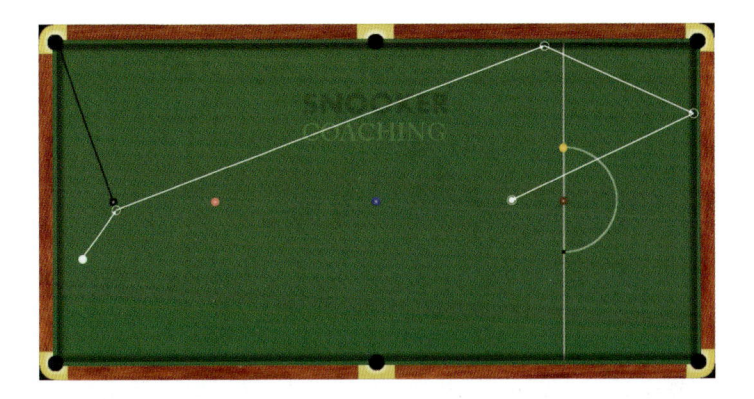

Following on from the shots in the previous lesson continue, but this time from the opposite side of the table.

Shots from the Opposite Side

Position 1 – This is just below Black, so strike a fraction above the middle to come off the side cushion for position on Yellow.

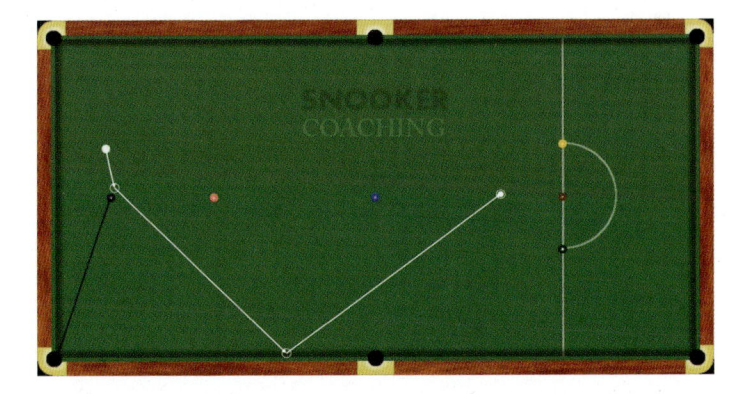

Position 2 – Slightly lower than position 1 becomes a run-through shot off the side cushion.

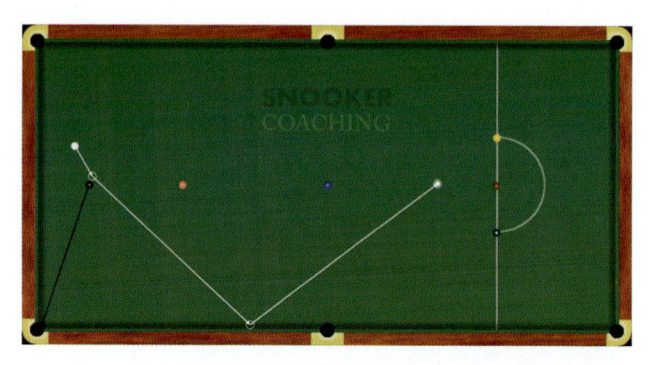

Position 3 – Lower still becomes a tough shot, so hit at 7 o'clock off the side and bottom cushion to go between Green and Brown for position on Yellow.

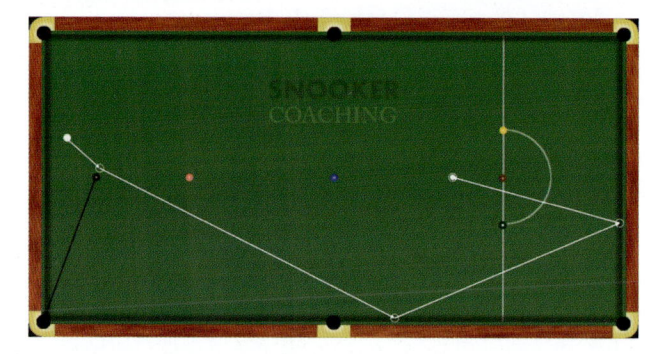

Screw with Reverse Side

Set the balls as illustrated.
Try to pot the Black and come off the side cushion.

Pink to Yellow Shots

Set the balls as illustrated.

Position 1 – This is from a straight position. Don't screw off the side cushion as it is possible you will go in off – just pot Pink and screw back 7 to 8 inches for long pot on Yellow.

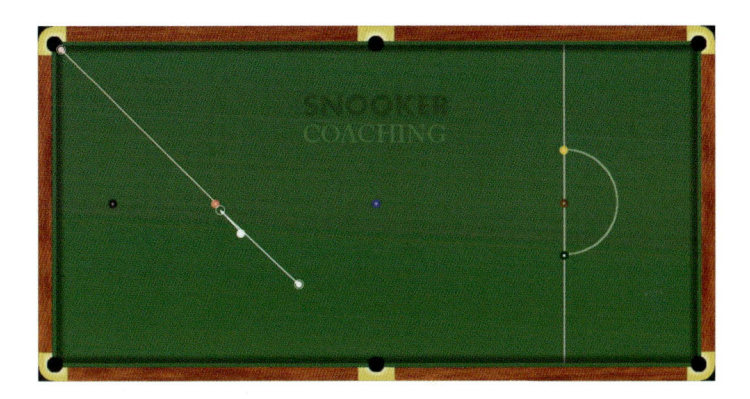

Position 2 – This is a 3/4 ball pot where you can screw back for position on Yellow.

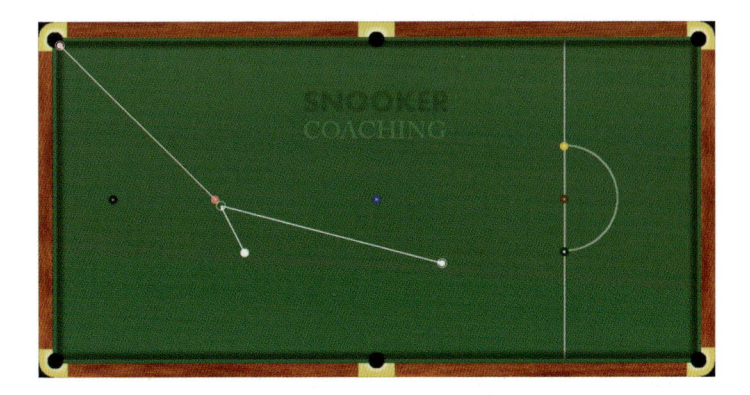

Position 3 – This is a 1/2 ball pot, so you need to stun off the side cushion for position on Yellow.

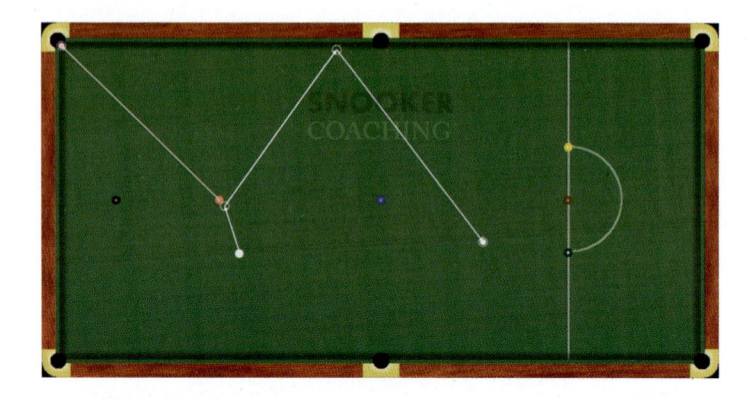

Position 4 – This is a 1/4 ball pot, so strike at 1 o'clock so the trace of side gives you position on Yellow.

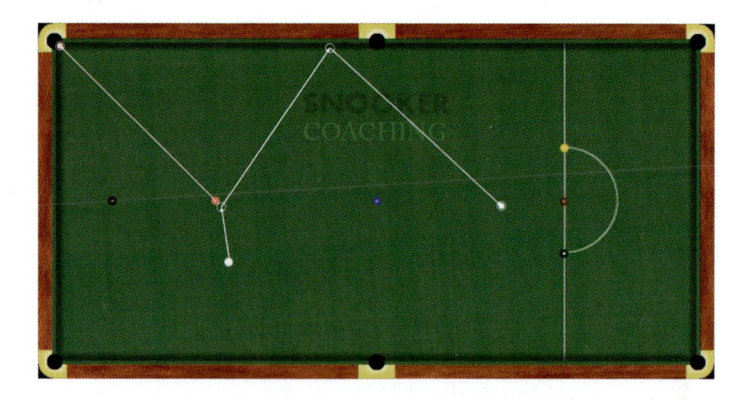

Following on from shots in the previous lesson, continue but this time from the other side of the table.

From the Opposite Side of the Table

Position 1 – This is a 3/4 ball pot where you can screw back for position on Yellow.

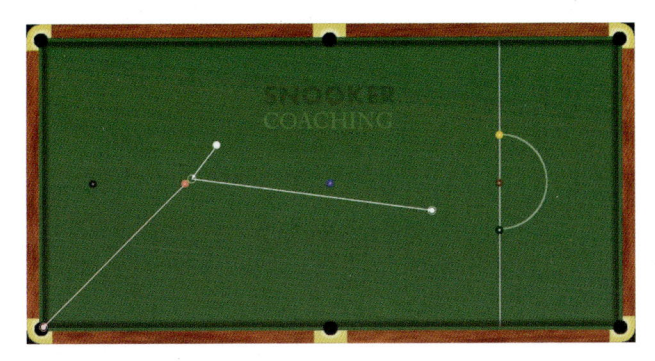

Position 2 – This is a 1/2 ball pot, so you need to stun off the side cushion for position on Yellow.

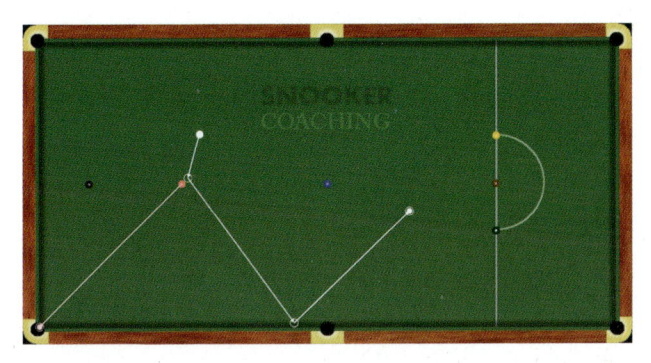

Position 3 – This is a 1/4 ball pot, so it's a run-through shot that gives you position on Yellow.

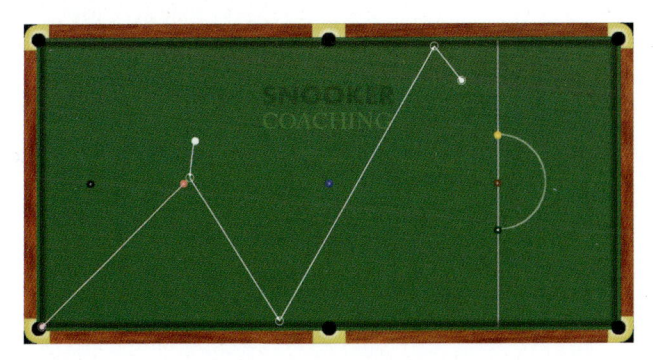

Following on from shots in the previous lesson, continue but this time from the other side of the table, and this is a slightly longer lesson as you have now reached the end of the formal lessons.

Pink to Yellow Continuation Shots

Set the balls as illustrated.

Position 1 – This is a 3/4 ball pot simply running through off the top cushion for position on Yellow.

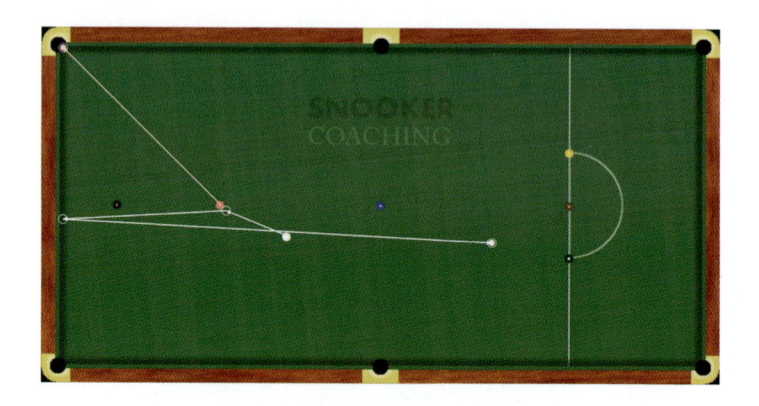

Position 2 – This is the same position as above, but you can also play this as a stun shot off the top and side cushion for position on Yellow.

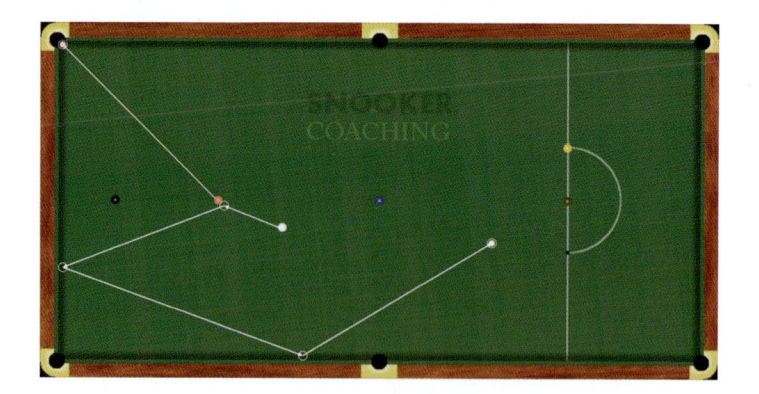

Position 3 – This is a 1/2 ball shot, striking the white at 11 o'clock to come off the top and side cushion for position on Yellow.

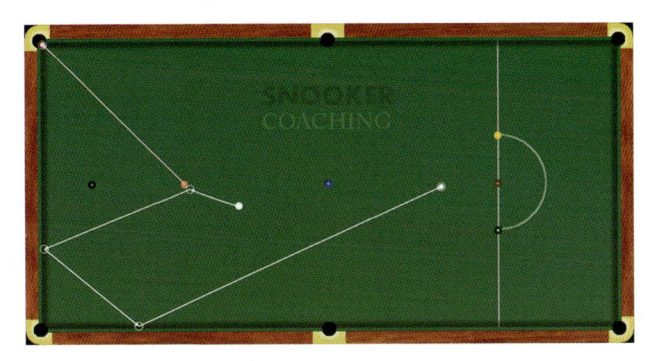

Position 4 – This is a 1/4 ball shot, so you will need the rest. No side needed to come off top and side cushions for position on Yellow.

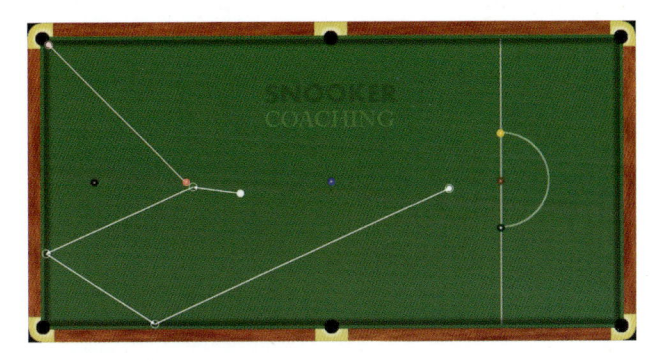

From the Opposite Side of the Table

Set the balls as illustrated.
　　Position 1 – This is a 3/4 ball pot using the rest to stun off the top and side for position on Yellow.

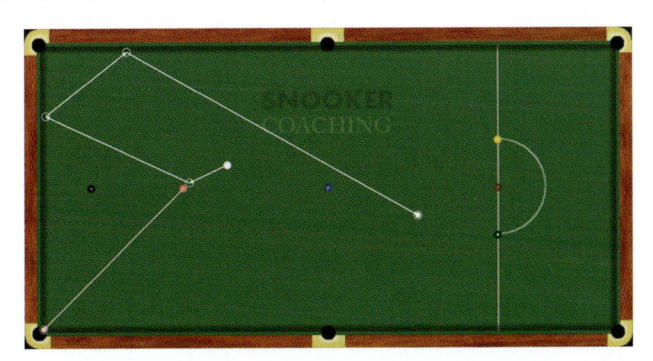

Position 2 – This is a 1/2 ball stun shot using the rest to come off the top and side cushion for position on Yellow. No side needed.

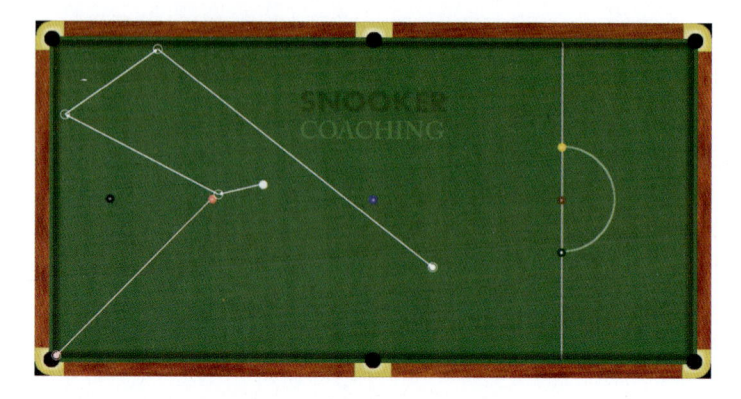

Position 3 – This is a 1/4 ball shot, so you will need the rest and strike at 1 o'clock to come off top and side cushions for position on Yellow.

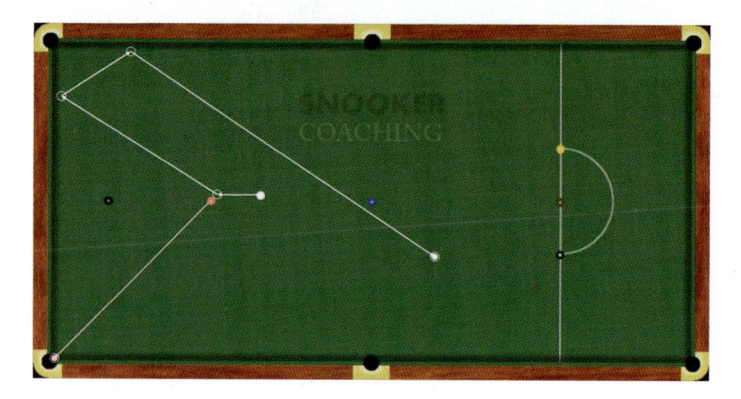

Index

1/4 Ball Double 98
3 Cushions and Back 39
6 Angles on Blue 45

Almost Straight 146
Almost Straight to Yellow 119
Angled Red 151

Back to Baulk 12, 38, 44
Ball and Cushion 95
Balls along the Cushion 155, 156
Baulk Line pots 48
Baulk Safety 51
Black Red Black 7
Black Safety 49
Black to Baulk Routine 11
Black to Black 22
Black to Yellow 29, 30, 115, 116, 136, 161, 164
Black with Screw 60
Black with Stun 59
Black with Top-Spin 59
Black, Screw, Black Routine 21
Blind-Pocket Pot 159
Blue and Stun to Pink 34
Blue Close Green 76
Blue from 3 Positions 105
Blue Split 101
Break-Off 73
Brown to Black 37, 138
Brown to Blue Shots 140, 141, 142, 143, 144

Cannon 3 Reds 36
Clearing the Colours 64
Cocked Hat Double 100
Cocked Hat Shot 93
Complete 15 Half-Ball Losers 18
Complete Shots 144
Controlling the Cue Ball 63

Cross Double 94, 99
Cross Double Safety 58, 135
Cross Red Safety 74
Cue Ball behind Black 50
Cut-Back Doubles 93

Developing Touch 72
Double to Baulk 38
Double to Middle 99

Easy Plant 104
Easy Safety 134
Escape 1 91
Escape 2 91
Escape 3 92
Escape 4 92
Escape Shot 154, 155

Final Clearance 68
From the Opposite Side of the Table 169, 171
Fun off the Pink 159

Green Split 31, 101
Green to Black 29

Half-Ball Black to Yellow 117
Half-Ball Potting 69
Half-Ball Safety off the Red 82
High on Blue 128, 129, 130

Key Shots on Brown 126

Long Browns 55
Long Pot 74
Long Range Baulk Safety 37
Long Red and Black 54
Long-Range Baulk Safety Routine 26
Loose Red 45

173

Nearside Pink 87

Off-Straight Pink 86
Off-Straight Pink Routine 16

Pack Split 31, 100
Pink and Run 87
Pink from 3 Positions 106
Pink from 5 Angles 46
Pink to Middle from 3 Positions 109
Pink to Yellow 34, 137
Pink to Yellow Continuation Shots 170
Pink to Yellow Shots 167
Pink, Stun, Black Routine 21
Play Safe off the Black 27
Position on Black from Green 135
Pot 20 Straight Pinks to Middle 12
Pot Almost Straight Blue to Middle 17
Pot and Cannon 137
Pot and Follow 133
Pot and Run 55, 160
Pot and Screw 32
Pot Black 58
Pot Black and Screw 132
Pot Black and Screw to the Cushion 33
Pot Black Left-Hand Side for Yellow 119
Pot Blue and Pink 83, 84
Pot Blue and Split the Pack 73, 82
Pot Blue and Stun to Brown 35
Pot Blue Run Through 25
Pot Blue with Stun/Side 26
Pot Brown and Stun to Blue 24, 35
Pot Green 66
Pot Green off its Spot with a Trace of Right Side 19
Pot Green using Follow, Side, Stun and Screw 24
Pot Pink and Black 132
Pot Red and Blue 88
Pot Red and Screw to Black 33
Pot Red Pot Black 8
Pot Red Stun to Black 36
Pot Yellow and Screw 23
Pot Yellow and Stun 23

Pot Yellow off its Spot with a Trace of Left Side 18
Pot Yellow with Side 22
Pots on the Brown Ball 41
Pots on Yellow 40
Potting Angles Blue to Middle Pocket 60
Potting Angles on Black into Corner Pocket 61
Potting the Yellow 7
Potting to the Middle 152
Power Run Through 149
Practice on Black 110
Pro Safety 121

Red on Black Spot 15
Red to Baulk Colours 62
Red/Blue/Colours 50
Red and Black 51
Red behind Black 49
Red Black Routine 8
Red off the Top Cushion 48
Red Right Over the Top Pocket 15
Red Screw to Black 53
Red Stun to Black 54
Reply to Safe Black 126
Re-Spotted Black Safety Shot 57
Rest Work 88
Roll Up Safety Shot 56
Roll Up to Red 95
Roll-Up Escape 94
Run through Green 89
Running Left 114

Safe and Sound 47
Safety 28
Safety – Cue Ball Behind Black 148
Safety – Loose Red
Safety – Red Behind Black 148
Safety – Red to Baulk 146
Safety – White Behind Black 149
Safety Double 147
Safety First Routine 46
Safety in Mind 47
Safety into the Pack 19

Safety into the Reds 76
Safety off a Tempting Red 83
Safety off Black 98, 125
Safety off Black 2 125
Safety off Blue 85
Safety off Green 84, 86
Safety off Pink 32, 85
Safety on Black 157
Safety Shot 77, 78, 79, 144, 145
Safety to Baulk 28
Safety to Colours 57
Safety to Side Cushion 52
Screw and Right 115
Screw off Cushion 90
Screw off Yellow 90
Screw Shot Control 62
Screw to Black 134
Screw to Pink 108
Screw with Reverse Side 166
Shot to Nothing 75, 96
Shots from the Opposite Side 162, 165
Shots on the Pink 131
Shots to Nothing 79, 80, 81
Slow Drag 56
Snooker Escape 113
Snooker off the Red 96
Soft Screw on Black 160
Split Pack 30 102
Splitting a Flat Pack 158
Splitting a Pack off the Back Cushion 158
Splitting the Pack off Baulk Colours 157
Squeezed Set 102
Stop Shot 39
Straight Long Blues 27

Straight on Black to Yellow 118
Stun and Run Routine 10
Stun and Side Black to Yellow 117
Stun off Brown 89
Stun Run 133
Stun to Black 53
Stun to Blue 14
Stun to Pink 108
Stun to Yellow from Black 118
Stun-Run 20
Stun-Run into D 61
Stun-Run Routine 9
Stun-Screw 20
Stun-Screw Routine 9
Swerve and Pot 77

T Set 103
Thin Red to Black Routine 52
Three Straight Reds with Screw Routine 13
Three Straight Reds with Top Routine 13
Top to Reds 10
Trace of Side 150
Trace of Side 2 150
Two Cushion Split 113

Useful Snooker Shot 112

Wider Angle on Blue 25
Wrong Side of Blue 114, 138
Wrong Side of Blue to Yellow 120, 121

Yellow into Pack 75
Yellow No Side Routine 14

ALSO AVAILABLE FROM CROWOOD

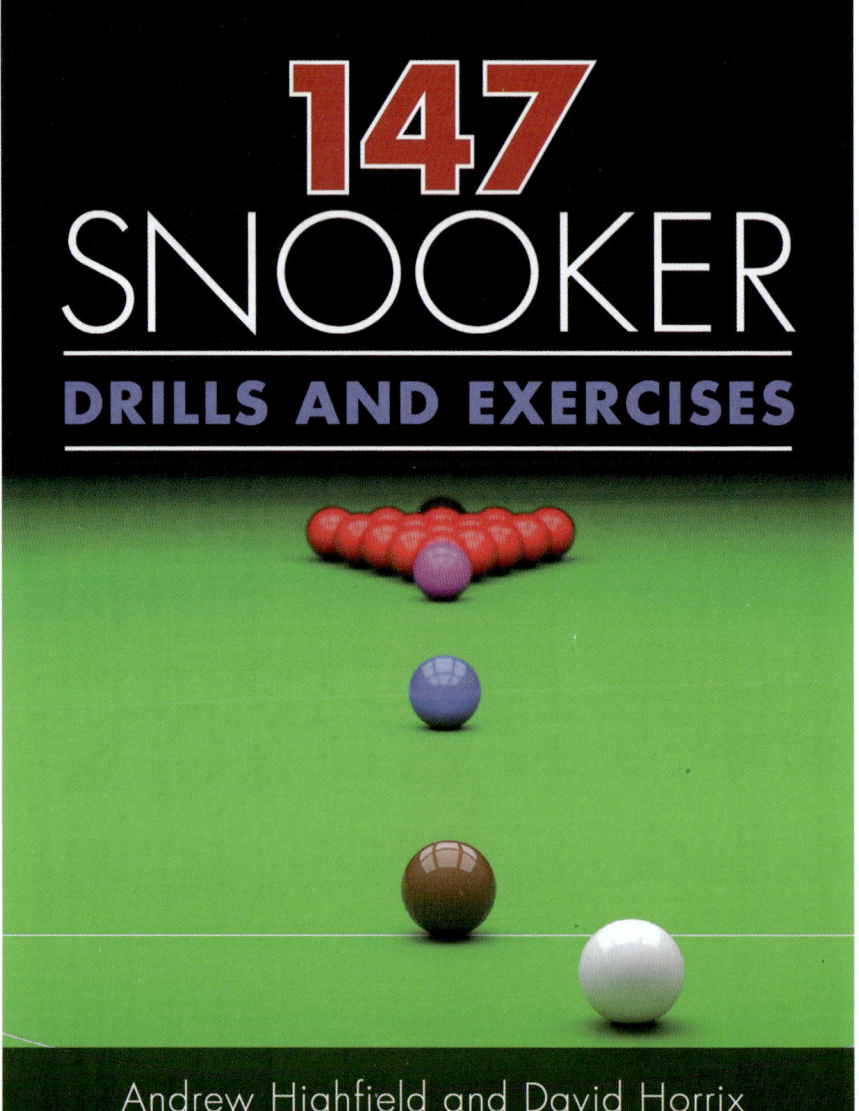

147 SNOOKER
DRILLS AND EXERCISES

Andrew Highfield and David Horrix